# Distributed Ledgers

# Distributed Ledgers
Design and Regulation of Financial
Infrastructure and Payment Systems

Robert M. Townsend

The MIT Press
Cambridge, Massachusetts
London, England

© 2020 Massachusetts Institute of Technology

This work is subject to a Creative Commons CC-BY-NC-ND license.

Subject to such license, all rights are reserved.

The open access edition of this book was made possible by generous funding from Arcadia—a charitable fund of Lisbet Rausing and Peter Baldwin.

This book was set in Sabon by Westchester Publishing Services. Printed and bound in the United States of America.

Library of Congress Cataloging-in-Publication Data

Names: Townsend, Robert M., 1948- author.
Title: Distributed ledgers : design and regulation of financial infrastructure and payment systems / Robert M. Townsend.
Description: Cambridge : The MIT Press, 2020. | Includes bibliographical references and index.
Identifiers: LCCN 2020004676 | ISBN 9780262539876 (paperback)
Subjects: LCSH: Financial services industry--Technological innovations.
Classification: LCC HG173 .T69 2020 | DDC 332/.042402855758--dc23
LC record available at https://lccn.loc.gov/2020004676

10  9  8  7  6  5  4  3  2

# Contents

Preface vii
Acknowledgments ix

1  Introduction  1
2  Economies, Obstacles, Welfare, and Measurement  23
3  Ledgers as Financial Accounts  31
4  E-Payments, E-Messages, and Trusted Third Parties in Payment Systems  49
5  Encryption  59
6  Smart Contracts: Contract Theory and Mechanism Design  77
7  Design Issues: Partitioned Ledgers, the Decision to Decentralize Implementation in Multiparty Contracts, and Incentive-Compatible Token Payment Systems  103
8  Building Financial Infrastructure on Distributed Ledgers: Practical Application in Emerging Markets  115
9  Payment Systems on Distributed Ledgers: Practical Applications  127

10 Regulation and the Use of Distributed Ledger Technology   133

11 Cryptocurrency: The Role and Value of Tokens in Economies with Distributed Ledger Systems   145

12 Summary and Conclusion   167

Notes   181
References   187
Index   207

# Preface

Distributed ledgers have the potential to transform economic organization and financial structure. Yet the subject is embroiled in controversy, hype, and terminological inconsistencies. Rather than get waylaid by alternative possible definitions of distributed ledgers (also known as decentralized ledgers), we focus more broadly on an economic analysis of what distributed ledgers can do. We proceed by analyzing key individual components. We also compare and contrast the economic framework with the frameworks of computer science and data management disciplines to clarify the technology and take steps to combine these disciplines.

The familiar but key components of distributed ledgers discussed in this book are ledgers as financial accounts, e-messages and e-value transfers, cryptography, and contracts including multiparty mechanisms. Each component is evaluated and illustrated through the context of historical and contemporary economies, with featured applications in both developed economies and emerging-market countries. These use cases are a hallmark of the book. A recurrent focus is the general equilibrium impact of innovations and welfare gains from innovations featuring key components. This does not require that all components be introduced at the same time.

Contract theory is used to derive optimal arrangements, constrained only by obstacles to trade, featuring how the various aspects of ledgers can deepen infrastructure. Mechanism design and monetary theory are used to study public versus partitioned ledgers and improvements in payment systems. Prudential regulation, rather than being a barrier to innovation, can be improved with the use of distributed ledger technologies.

The goal is to provide blueprints for the ex ante optimal design and regulation of financial systems, including not only choices at the end points of the spectrum—of centralized versus decentralized systems, as in the hype—but the choice of hybrid forms in between. Each key component is assessed from both computer science and economic perspectives, and syntheses are offered. Overall, the book provides a vision for where we are heading, being clear about obstacles along the way.

# Acknowledgments

I gratefully acknowledge research support from the Eunice Kennedy Shriver National Institute of Child Health and Human Development (NICHD), grant number R01 HD027638; the Centre for Economic Policy Research (CEPR) and the Department for International Development (DFID) under grant MRG002_1255; and funding assistance for the continuation of the field surveys by the Thailand Research Fund, the Bank of Thailand, and the University of Thai Chamber of Commerce. I also am grateful for the collaborations with the Federal Reserve Banks of New York, Boston, and Chicago; Lightnet for its decentralized settlement banking network; and EvryNet for the decentralized custodian banking network in Thailand. The views expressed are my own. Thank you to Ernst-Ludwig von Thadden, James McAndrews, discussants of this work, and other participants at the Sveriges Riksbank Annual Macroprudential Conference in June 2017; participants at the Kellogg Conference on Development Economics at Northwestern University in September 2018; participants at the Cryptocurrencies and Blockchains Conference at the Becker Friedman Institute in November 2018; participants at the First New York Fed Conference on FinTech, March 2019; participants at the Penn State Conference in Celebration of Neil Wallace's Contribution to Economics, April 2019; Daniel Aronoff, Neha Narula, Neil Wallace, Joshua Gans, and Jesus

Fernandez-Villaverde for their very helpful comments; and Deborah Jamiol, Jennifer Roche, and Emily Gallagher for wonderful editing. Thank you also for comments on preliminary drafts to Marios Angeletos, Pablo Aznar, Zach Chao, Co-Pierre Georg, Michael Lee, Rhys Lindmark, Jacky Mallett, Antoine Martin, Nish Patel, and Nicolas Zhang. The reviewers for MIT Press made substantive contributions.

# 1
# Introduction

Distributed ledger technology (DLT) or, better put, its various features in isolation and in combination, has the potential to be transformative. Nevertheless, this subject has engendered controversy and sharp debate as well as a lack of clarity in the terminology researchers use to discuss it.

The first part of this introduction outlines the debate, and the second part outlines the point of view of this book.

Of note, Bitcoin is thought of as having created the blockchain as part of its validation system, so some people consider Bitcoin, blockchain, and distributed ledger technology to be synonymous. They are not. Some distributed ledger technologies exist without the blockchain technology and without coins. Indeed, much of the technology for distributed ledgers existed before Bitcoin and blockchain.

So this book proceeds in reverse. It starts with distributed ledgers, works backward to blockchain, and defers a more in-depth discussion of cryptocurrencies to the end. Concepts, definitions, applications, and impact are discussed at each turn. The term "distributed ledger" is sometimes used synonymously (if incorrectly) with the term decentralization. Computer science and data science are needed to clarify the distinction, and we compare and contrast with the meaning of decentralization in economics.

## 1.1 General Motivation: A View from All Sides

We begin with selected quotes from policymakers and academics (not practitioners or fintechs) in support of the premise that technology is fundamental.

> DLT refers to *the processes and related technologies that enable nodes in a network (or arrangement) to securely propose, validate, and record state changes (or updates) to a synchronized ledger that is distributed across the network's nodes*. In the context of payment, clearing, and settlement, DLT enables entities, through the use of established procedures and protocols, to carry out transactions without necessarily relying on a central authority to maintain a single "golden copy" of the ledger.
>
> DLT may radically change how assets are maintained and stored, obligations are discharged, contracts are enforced, and risks are managed. Proponents of the technology highlight its ability to transform financial services and markets by: (i) reducing complexity; (ii) improving end-to-end processing speed and thus availability of assets and funds; (iii) decreasing the need for reconciliation across multiple record-keeping infrastructures; (iv) increasing transparency and immutability in transaction record keeping; (v) improving network resilience through distributed data management; and (vi) reducing operational and financial risks [Mills 2016]. DLT may also enhance market transparency if information contained on the ledger is shared broadly with participants, authorities and other stakeholders.
>
> —Bank for International Settlements (BIS 2017a, 2, 1)

> Contracts, transactions, and the records of them are among the defining structures in our economic, legal, and political systems. They protect assets and set organizational boundaries. They establish and verify identities and chronicle events. They govern interactions among nations, organizations, communities, and individuals. They guide managerial and social action. And yet these critical tools and the bureaucracies formed to manage them have not kept up with the economy's digital transformation. They're like a rush-hour gridlock trapping a Formula 1 race car.... With blockchain, we can imagine a world in which contracts are embedded in digital

code and stored in transparent, shared databases, where they are protected from deletion, tampering, and revision. In this world every agreement, every process, every task, and every payment would have a digital record and signature that could be identified, validated, stored, and shared.
—Marco Iansiti and Karim R. Lakhani, *Harvard Business Review*, 2017 (119–120)

But, of course, there are concerns and qualifications. We note some of these immediately, from the same sources. The Bank for International Settlements (BIS 2017a) lists risks associated with using DLT for payments that include potential uncertainty about operational and security issues arising from the technology; the lack of interoperability with existing processes and infrastructures; ambiguity relating to settlement finality; questions regarding the soundness of the legal underpinning for DLT implementations; absence of an effective and robust governance framework; and issues related to data integrity, immutability, and privacy. The Committee on Payments and Market Infrastructures (CPMI) chair, Benoît Cœuré, writes,

> Central banks have traditionally played an important catalyst role in payments and settlements. This report will help central banks, other authorities, and the public to identify the risks as well as the benefits associated with the emerging technology, which could be the basis for next-generation systems (BIS 2017b).[1]

Iansiti and Lakhani (2017) focus on the difficulty of adoption of transformative technologies. They distinguish between novelty and complexity, laying out various historical examples of innovation and current, ongoing experiments in DLT, in the end dividing innovations into four categories along the lines of high/low novelty and high/low complexity. This allows them to make predictions about not only where innovations are likely to succeed first, but also to identify those that could take considerable time, possibly decades, if they happen at all.

An implicit point: There is a distinction between invention of something new and its actual innovation and implementation. Lags in adoption are a murky criterion to use in the evaluation of the merits of inventions. This conflates the search for something "new" in DLT. Relatedly, innovation depends on context. In some settings, innovation is on the margin with much of the technology already in place. This may make the value of innovation marginal, potentially not worth the cost. But even if the gains from innovation could be incrementally large, vested interests with legacy systems can block change. In contrast, innovation can happen in settings where there is little if anything already in place on the ground, in which case implementation of key components singly, or in combination, can make a huge difference, even for innovations that are mundane and already adopted in other contexts.

An example of a low novelty–low complexity innovation given by Iansiti and Lakhani (2017) is Bitcoin. Their argument is that Bitcoin is another object like money for the transfer of value—hence, nothing novel. This, however, belies both Bitcoin's creative algorithm and the controversy around it. To some, Bitcoin is singularly innovative. This has a lot to do with differences between computer scientists' and economists' perspectives, which we seek to clarify in this book. For others, Bitcoin is extremely problematic (we will return to this debate shortly). In any event, the bulk of innovations and experiments in new technologies occur under what Iansiti and Lakhani refer to as "localization." That is, they introduce highly innovative uses and products but with a limited number of users. The list of these types of localized technologies is growing in length, some moving beyond commitments to experimentation and actual implementation.

One DLT use case that immediately reveals what DLT can do involves land-title projects such as those in Georgia, Sweden, and the Ukraine (Reese 2017). To buy property in these locations, the lawful owner must have a secure title to sign over to the purchaser. DLT uses hashes to record every real-estate transaction and make them immutable, publicly available, and searchable so that titles can be transferred quickly, without costly title searches. Propy.com is an example of a proprietary company innovating in this space, with a distributed ledger in active use. The same idea underlies the emergence of digital assets to facilitate ownership and transfer.

In practice, in many markets, there are gaps and pauses in transaction time lines even for the most obvious transactions. A key example: In financial markets, trade, clearing, and settlement are separated in time. An agreement to trade between two parties can happen quickly, but it is then recorded into the private and proprietary legacy systems of each party, hence requiring reconciliation later. Trades in equity on a central stock exchange can take two days or more to settle, and, in part, this is not a matter of choice as there is no immutable synchronized record on which all parties can rely. Digital Asset is a company that has entered into an agreement with the Australian stock exchange to allow trade and confirmation in equities in real time, which was scheduled to be in operation by 2020.

TReDS, in India, is a platform for the discounting and sale of trade receivables. There are two other competing platforms currently operating in India. Since 2017, these three platforms have been operating a common distributed ledger for the recording of submitted buyer-seller receivable transactions. Each transaction has a unique ID number, so there can be no duplicates and thus no fraud. The Hong Kong Monetary Authority is also implementing a DLT system to avoid double invoicing.

Stellar is a not-for-profit entity that Iansiti and Lakhani would place in the category of an innovation with low novelty and high coordination needs. Stellar focuses on banking, micropayments, and remittances for people without access to the formal financial sector or those who have access but at a high cost. Stellar has been operating since late 2014 and has a current market valuation, at the time of writing, of $2 billion. Ripple is a for-profit entity with an even larger valuation, $13.5 billion, founded in 2012. Stellar emerged from Ripple.

There is also innovation in nonfinancial markets. In 2017, Maersk and IBM implemented a distributed ledger technology for freight shipping, both for tracking and for improved logistics, sharing information and documentation among connecting nodes: port and terminal operators, customs authorities, customs brokers, transportation companies, and cargo owners. They project a substantial reduction in shipping costs.[2] Walmart has partnered with IBM to develop a system to track the supply chain of leafy vegetables from farms to stores so that in case of contamination, Walmart can quickly pinpoint and pull suspect produce. There are many such projects at the prototype stage—for example, pharmaceutical blockchain for reliable drugs.

Regarding smart contracts, Iansiti and Lakhani (2017) assign them to the most innovative yet hardest-to-implement category. Ethereum, R3's Corda, and Hyperledger are examples of smart-contract technologies running on distributed ledgers. As an example, Universal Market Access (UMA) allows contracts in financial derivatives that pay off as a function of the price of underlying assets.

One should be cognizant of the hype in the field and the difficulty of getting accurate, up-to-date information. There is continued discussion of improvement of the trade, clearing, and settlement systems at the Depository Trust and Clearing Corporation (DTCC) for repurchase agreements (repos) in the New York financial market—critical to the execution of the Federal Reserve's monetary policy. The reconciliation process takes up to two hours every trading day, creating an obvious friction. Yet the announced agreement between DTTC and

Digital Asset to install DLT did not move forward. One view is that a consensus in syndicates with conflicting interests is difficult to achieve, especially with existing infrastructure in place. A second view is that the proposed system added infrastructure on top of the old, adding to complexity and costs. In contrast to these negative experiences, DTCC and 15 leading global banks, in collaboration with IBM and Axoni, are implementing a re-platformed version of its Trade Information Warehouse for credit derivatives using synchronized distributed ledgers.

The Maersk platform is criticized by some as being proprietary to Maersk and apparently has had difficulty attracting other major shipping companies, arguably for that reason. This too is an increasingly typical experience, an obstacle recognized by participants in the industry. Surfing the web, a nontrivial set of initiatives seems to pitch blockchain, and billions of dollars are being spent on development, yet DLT may be pushed where there may be little need (Columbus 2019).

Controversy seems intrinsic to the technology or, better put, intrinsic to the way it is sometimes pitched. Observers draw an analogy between DLT today and the distributed computer networking technology known as TCP/IP (transmission control protocol/internet protocol), which is the communication protocol that laid the groundwork for the development of the internet. Following Iansiti and Lakhani (2017) closely, before TCP/IP, bilateral connections between two parties or machines had to be preestablished and sustained throughout an exchange, which was achieved though billions of dedicated communication lines. In contrast, TCP/IP transmitted information by digitizing it, breaking it up into very small packets, releasing it into the network, and finally, with smart receiving nodes, reassembling the packets and interpreting the encoded data. TCP/IP created an open, shared public network without any central authority or single party responsible for its maintenance and improvement.

This idyllic vision is maintained by many in the computer science research community and in industry and permeates the websites and white papers describing new releases. There are, by now, hundreds of cryptocurrencies and various leading platforms for the exchange of digital assets.[3] Nevertheless, there are concerns and qualifications worthy of emphasis here.

First, the computer science community recognizes that there are trade-offs in the design of communication, computation, and decision-making systems: limited capacity in communication, latency (time lags) in transmission, and especially interpretation of information received (Mallett 2009). These trade-offs are not necessarily taken into account in some discussions of validation systems, but they are an intrinsic part of such systems. The synchronization of so-called decentralized ledgers actually requires centralization or coordination across nodes, and this is costly. Arguably, the validation systems of Ripple and Stellar arose to deal with some of these problems in Bitcoin, which is slow and done by blocks, not only to economize on costly proof of work but to deal with network latency (Hinzen, John, and Saleh 2019).

Likewise, hierarchical top-down systems do have some virtues, as in military command-and-control systems. Often, an optimizing choice would be a hybrid in between, which is hard to describe as either decentralized or hierarchical. The point is that there are trade-offs and choices that depend on context and goals.[4] This is the interesting challenge of design. More generally, the language used to describe DLT, as if decentralized, is misleading. The term "disintermediation," in its most favorable light, means, presumably, the elimination of the profits of financial intermediaries and market makers. Yet the financial platforms of fintechs and liquid high-velocity financial assets accomplish financial intermediation by almost any reasonable definition economists could use.

Second, the phrase "absence of a central authority" naturally creates controversy among policymakers. Specifically, as stated in the Bitcoin white paper written under the alias Satoshi Nakamoto (2008, 1): "What is needed is an electronic payment system based on cryptographic proof instead of trust, allowing any two willing parties to transact directly with each other without the need for a trusted third party." Or, to put this crudely and more provocatively, the aim is to create a payment system that eliminates the need for central banks in the provision of money. Denison, Lee, and Martin (2016) make the point that, with exceptions, people do trust third parties: Both central banks that provide currency and reserves and (derivative) payment systems run by the named and trusted institutions that maintain the ledgers and operating systems.[5]

In what follows we will highlight hybrid systems where some of the features of distributed ledgers allow useful innovation, while other parts of the same systems rely on trusted third parties. It is the view of this book that neither side of the debate should dismiss these hybrids on the grounds they do not qualify as DLTs under some overly stringent definition.

## 1.2 Methods and Philosophy

To lay out the point of view of this book more specifically, we start, first, with the premise: Technological improvements in the design of mediation/intermediation systems could potentially, if executed properly, allow economies to be more connected in a positive way. Connectedness can come from new forms of mediation, though, as is already evident, not necessarily traditional intermediation through existing formal-sector financial institutions. Rather, the idea is (or should be) to create needed missing markets and institutions to fill in gaps in financial access and reduce inefficiencies, some of which are large. Technological change is not new per se; we have witnessed various historical episodes of innovation. Communication systems have evolved from oral assignment to paper recording and written messages to e-messages and electronic registries (Townsend 1990; 1987). These episodes are instructive, as some of the basics of these episodes are the same as those observed in the current wave of DLT advanced communication and recording systems. These episodes of innovation also serve the purpose of allowing us to step back from the hype and controversy of DLT in order to highlight its key components and welfare gains.

Again, this book distinguishes invention from innovation. Was Bitcoin, with its blockchain and distributed ledgers, a sharply defined invention so that we can imagine innovations are now possible that were not possible before? Or was Bitcoin an innovation of previous inventions, a part of a longer, slow-moving process? The latter, for sure. Bitcoin with DLT was incremental. Nick Szabo described a decentralized digital currency, bit gold, with a public ledger and cryptographic puzzles a decade earlier (Moskov 2018; Narayanan et al. 2016). Szabo (1998) is also thought of as the originator of the smart contract implemented on distributed ledgers. Indeed, some argue that Szabo is Nakamoto, though he denies this.

Also relevant here are advances in database management and distributed computing, dating from years earlier. Secure multiparty computation goes back to the late 1970s, not simply to conceal content but also to conceal partial information about data while computing with data from many sources to produce publicly correct output. At least two of the key components of DLT, ledgers and cryptography, are so familiar to us that they seem mundane. Furthermore, some of these components have very deep historical roots dating back hundreds or thousands of years.

Nevertheless, there are recent, important, and contemporaneous innovations using these familiar components that have seen large welfare gains.[6] Likewise, there remain gaps to fill. This book seeks to make these potential welfare gains and gaps transparent by being explicit about economic frictions and technological capabilities. It gives blueprints for the design of markets and institutions using suitably implemented components of distributed ledger technology, which includes formalizations of the limits of communication and database management systems widely discussed in the computer science literature.

On the negative side are bugs and troubling episodes. Consider the disturbing hacking event involving the Decentralized Autonomous Organization (DAO), a smart contract on Ethereum Classic. A hacker found a loophole in the coding and drained the equivalent of $70 million in Ether cryptocurrency in the first few hours of the attack (Falkon 2017). The subsequent fork between Ethereum and Ethereum Classic also illustrates that smart contracts are not necessarily immutable after all, begging larger questions about consensus and legal frameworks. There has been apparent fraud in cryptocurrency exchanges. Largely unregulated at first, the Securities and Exchange Commission in the United States has argued that tokens are securities, though there is no regulatory consensus. On the other hand, it is not clear that traditional regulatory frameworks are appropriate either, revealing a gap in understanding that this book also tries to fill.

The conceptual framework adopted here is that of general equilibrium, and the welfare metric for deciding if something is good or bad, as well as how it should be regulated, is the Pareto criterion for a given economy. The recommended way of proceeding with this artillery is to assess what can be accomplished in a given economy relative to what is there now and, more specifically (at least in some contexts), exactly how to innovate.

Indeed, we can distinguish three possible metrics for this assessment of what can be accomplished, which, as a warning, can be easily confounded with one other. One would be to reduce obstacles to exchange and mitigate frictions. A second is to place value on products/systems that are commercially viable and actually potentially profitable. The third is again our basic standard: to allow allocations that are Pareto improvements relative to previous outcomes, though losers may need to be compensated. These metrics are not always equivalent with each other. One reason for failures of equivalence comes from the potential failure of the first fundamental welfare theorem in economics. The theorem states that under certain assumptions any competitive equilibrium, decentralized through a price system, must be Pareto optimal. But under some frictions, competitive equilibrium allocations are not necessarily Pareto optimal, and potential failures are intimately associated with some of the properties of e-money as money more generally. Another reason for failure is the political economy of reform. There can be losers from removing an obstacle, especially if there is no compensation, as noted. This may also explain slow adoption or failure to innovate even when the technology is well understood and potentially Pareto improving.

A broader view also comes naturally with mechanism design, where the distinction between public and private ownership has no real meaning. Agents enter into social agreements, subject to information, resources, and other constraints. It is as if a "planner" were acting on behalf of agents as a collective group. But the word "planner" is a misnomer, especially in this book as we sort through language issues. A planner would refer to a highly centralized system, juxtaposed with autonomous decentralized markets. Here, the planner of mechanism design theory acts through a secure multiparty computation framework in which underlying states are not required to be revealed. We will revisit this issue later, in particular how to compute and implement optimized solutions to multiparty smart contracts and the limitations in doing so.

A counterexample to a forced distinction between private and public ownership is the case of private clearinghouses as a consortium of financial institutions—an industry association with tight rules for membership, collateral, and operations. Clearinghouses were not always connected to central bank accounts for settlement (Tucker 2014) and yet were public institutions in many ways. Campbell-Kelly (2010) describes the Bankers Clearing House in Britain and, with modifications, the Clearing House of New York, as algorithms for netting and settlement of checks among bankers, implemented by humans rotating around tables rather than computers yet sharing much with the code and liquidity issues of contemporaneous e-payment systems.[7]

The book proceeds, then, as outlined here. This introduction serves as an executive summary and the final chapter reviews the context again while also attempting to draw some conclusions from our analysis.

Chapter 2 describes the concept of what we mean by an economy: the underlying commodity space, general enough to include time, uncertainty, and geography. All the examples in this book fit into this general framework. The welfare criterion is made clear. When additional information and other constraints are appended onto programming problems for the determination of the class of optimal allocations, we refer to the solutions as *constrained optimal*. Measurement is also featured, ideally with integrated financial accounts, if available. We present the Townsend Thai project as an example of an economy, and it appears repeatedly though the chapters as a source of examples, chosen because many of the ingredients we wish to discuss come together there.

Chapters 3 through 6 describe four key components of distributed ledgers: ledgers as accounts, e-messages and e-value transfers, cryptography, and contracts including multiparty mechanisms. We discuss, evaluate, and illustrate through the context of historical and contemporary economies each component, with featured applications in both developed economies and emerging-market countries. A recurrent focus is the general equilibrium impact of innovations and welfare gains from innovations featuring these key components, which does not require that all components be introduced at the same time.

Specifically, chapter 3 introduces ledgers in the context of various emerging markets and advanced economies. The ledgers are linked to statements of currency flows in Thailand as a first example, showing conceptually how common yet distributed accounts could be created from a database of transactions at the level of households and small and medium-sized enterprises (SMEs). One gain from a common database is that discrepancies in entries across agents can be detected and, in principle, corrected as they occur. There is an analogy with how financial accounts and double-entry bookkeeping allow for greater accuracy at the individual level. Illustrative applications of the use of financial accounts indicate new and important uses for the application of distributed ledgers.

This section on ledgers concludes with an important discussion from the computer science literature on the advantages and disadvantages of traditional database management versus the decentralized database management of distributed ledgers. With decentralization, in the presence of latency, impossibility theorems arise with regard to consistency (ledgers the same), accuracy (up-to-date and without error), and partition tolerance (in the presence of a partition tolerance, one has to choose between consistency and availability). Furthermore, even when the system is running normally, there is a tension between consistency and latency. From the distributed computing literature there is a theorem that with asynchronous systems, consensus is impossible. Yet with synchronous systems each node must be connected to every other node and thus, with communication costs, this raises the issue of scaling up to large systems. Trusted third parties solve this problem, but this centralization not only requires trust but raises the issue of data integrity, as those with the correct access can also (accidentally) destroy or corrupt data, and there is data security/cyber-risk. In practice, choices are made and hybrids emerge.

Roughly speaking, database management systems have not paid much attention to incentives among parties with conflicting interests. Distributed ledgers for business applications err toward keeping everything secret, not toward solving a design problem. In this book we thus point an arrow toward where we could go. An example from economics with transactions costs from linking provides an illustration of an optimal hybrid system.

Chapter 4 features the second component: e-messages and e-payments. We compare and contrast examples of e-money, looking at Thailand, with its dominant use of paper currency and little e-value transfer, and at Sweden, where the use of e-payments now dominates and the use of currency has fallen off tremendously. This sets the stage for understanding an e-money innovation with large welfare gains: the case of M-Pesa through the mobile company Safaricom in Kenya. Many low-income and developing countries could experience such welfare gains. The Kenyan system uses a trusted third party and so what is to some a defining characteristic of DLT, no trusted third party, might lead one to dismiss this innovation. Alternatively, the gains from the e-transfer component are large with trusted parties. However, there are several caveats. Trust is less obvious when one takes into account the larger financial system. In addition, there are some infrastructure issues and the provision of liquidity that deserve attention in these contexts.

Chapter 5 deals with cryptography, validation, and consensus. A description of how contemporaneous e-systems work without a universal trusted third party does beg the issue of consensus. However, there is no one single way to achieve consensus. Among the various consensus systems are Bitcoin cryptography with proof of work, Byzantine fault tolerant systems with proof of stake and voting rights based on coin ownership, and federated Byzantine protocols with layers of trust. There are trade-offs across these systems that involve fault tolerance, safety/consistency, liveness, latency, and transaction speed. Bitcoin and consensus algorithms have attracted much of the academic and industry interest, and there are interesting issues being revealed as computer scientists, economists, and their literatures interact. In addition, chapter 5 explores the validation systems and economics of Ripple, Stellar, Algorand, and HotStuff, the basis for Libra.

Chapter 6 presents the fourth component, contracts and multi-agent arrangements that are implemented as smart contracts. This chapter includes a discussion of how contract and mechanism design theory delineate various distinct concepts of trust, thus helping to clarify the debate concerning trusted third parties and what is needed, or not. Smart contracts operate on distributed ledgers and overcome obstacles—namely, there is commitment in entering into an agreement and in carrying it out (the immutability of terms). The language is similar to that used in financial accounting, with states for the balance sheet and flows as in cash flow, executed with commands. There are hybrid smart-contact systems with lots of possibilities and flexibility: unique and nonunique consensus; single or multiple trusting or nontrusted notaries; public versus private nodes; oracles for public information; and broadcast versus selectively private communication. The contracts and mechanisms that economists envision to deal with specified obstacles and frictions in an environment now have DLT as a natural implementation technology.

Basics include messages sent and recording on the ledger; truth telling and hence no further verification; past messages recorded as immutable history; enduring relationships under multi-period contacts; promised utilities as the key summary of past history; incentives to take appropriate actions; utility threats for lying about past history; costly state verification with no messages over a range of states; full commitment versus limited commitment distinguishing one meaning of trust; reneging and thus a restriction to time consistency or the building of an internal scoring reputation mechanism; collusion and remedies for implementation; and commitment to limit sequential play to solve hold-up and bargaining problems.

In chapter 6 there is also a discussion of the similarities and differences between economics and computer science, including some concluding comments on integration. In much of computer science, nodes are trusted or not, and designs center around having a sufficient number of trusted nodes, as in fault tolerance. Yet smart contracts for mechanism design problems, if entirely implemented on Ethereum with its proof of work, including validation of code, can be prohibitively costly. Messages internal to the contract might also be done on-chain, but this is largely unnecessary if we respect internal incentives. Likewise, databases and documents can be secured off-chain. There is, however, encouraging common ground. Costly and imperfect messaging can be incorporated into the mechanism design, or even no messages at all, yet versions of the revelation principle still apply in some contexts. Though there are impossibility results regarding consensus and common knowledge in the economics literature, one can build on this and draw a distinction between following naïve or simple communication protocols versus incentives and strategic behavior in well-defined economic games. Optimal design of communication systems thus becomes key. Recent contributions establish the effectiveness of multiple repeat messages and how iterations of decentralized validation can be truncated to achieve coordination. These are the nuts and bolts we need going forward.

Chapter 7 builds on smart contracts, going on to explore issues in "decentralization." In some environments it is necessary to partition ledgers so that messages are sent but not seen by everyone, which improves incentives. Likewise, ultimate outcomes are randomized to facilitate concealment, which improves constrained risk-sharing. There is also a discussion of the need in some environments to have a preprogrammed, third-party custodian making portfolio decisions. Another consideration is how the burden of validation can be lessened if there are portable, concealable tokens that can be carried about and displayed voluntarily on request. A system that records histories of trade—which DLT provides—can improve welfare relative to a decentralized, partitioned system in which information is lost. Indeed, in a hybrid decentralized system, tokens can play a distinct role in implementing the centralized mechanism design outcome by conveying histories of trades—a kind of communication system, but one that avoids problems of scale. This can provide insurance and smoothing over time, even if tokens, or line items on ledgers, could in principle be concealed. Incentives for revelation of tokens or revelation of private accounts take care of that problem. The messages are endogenous, not forced or required as under centralized systems, but the messages are fully revealing. Tokens can also be used to track trades over multiple commodities, such as when there are preference shocks, but here, multiple colored coins may be needed if there are multiple dimensions to keep track of, for example, if over time there are shocks associated with preference reversals. This has a parallel in cryptography: Coins are not fungible, in the sense that coins have publicly verified histories, to trace ownership.

Several chapters deal with specific applications. The Thai setting is featured in chapter 8, making the point that context matters. Large gaps in services exist for credit, savings, payments, and insurance (Asian Development Bank 2017). The Townsend Thai project, on the ground with 20 years of data, shows that informal, local risk-sharing is good, achieved through credit chains and networks. But there are shortfalls in cash management. There are also shortfalls in county-level risk-sharing. The risk premium is low for idiosyncratic risk because of good pooling. Yet the risk premium is high for aggregate risk, even though aggregates differ across villages and could be pooled and better insured. Interventions have helped, but more are needed. A government village fund intervention allowed increased consumption overall by alleviating borrowing constraints and a cashing in of buffer stocks; better intermediation, especially for the lower-wealth households, through a costly state verification regime, with lower costs of verification for kin; and profits and increases in assets for high-productivity SMEs that received funds. But loans were more readily available for village committee members and those with connections to them; some kinship pathways mitigated distortions, but evidently these rely on preexisting trust. High-productivity SMEs without kin could have benefited more. Smart contracts on distributed ledgers can help overcome some of these trust issues, allowing trade among strangers.

The point is that innovations that make use of distributed ledgers have great potential. There are gains from individual contracts and services, such as escrow services with nonbanks, savings products for automated deposit and portfolio management, and securitized waterfall payments along the path of supply chains from buyer to seller to employee loans. There are also gains from competition, because a common platform can provide structure for competition in contracts with open access to providers writing smart contracts, as with free entry in general equilibrium models with an intermediary broker sector. A featured example of innovation is EvryNet, an intelligent financial automation operation system that provides open-source banking services and financial contracts to unbanked and underbanked populations.

Chapter 9 turns to systems for actual or pending payments and describes two innovations on distributed ledgers. One was run as an experiment by a central bank for commercial banks in an advanced country, Project Jasper in Canada, and is replete with sophisticated algorithms implemented as smart, multiparty contracts for queuing and clearing. The other application embraces the full set of possibilities for payment systems designed to achieve constrained-optimal trade, credit, and insurance in the context of cross-border payments among money transfer operators (MTOs) in Southeast Asia. Lightnet features an optimized liquidity management layer that efficiently searches for offsetting cross-country fiat balances for expedient clearing. MTOs can be viewed as agents with varying income and balance sheets hit by shocks, with the need for trade for their customers, hence themselves needing credit and insurance. Velo Labs acts in conjunction with a digital reserve bank.

Chapter 10 deals with regulation as an integral part of financial system design using distributed ledgers. Each section in this chapter is separate from the others, with important ideas for actual uses. First, DLT can improve on the current technology used by banks and markets in order to mitigate, if not eliminate, resulting runs. The idea is to exploit the time-stamped and immutable nature of ledgers to keep track of history and to condition current outcomes. Second, competition among providers can fail to complete the financial system because of unexploited complementarities and lack of coordination. Traditional regulation by sector and product can exacerbate this problem. The time line of when to allow competition also matters. Not all forms of competition are good. Ex ante competition in rights to provide services and contracts can be fine, but there needs to be exclusivity and restrictions on contract execution and ex post spot trade. DLT systems can provide these, in principle.

The last section of chapter 10 shows that, in some instances, public information on ledgers is necessary for coordination and prudential regulation. To achieve an optimum, one has to know where the system is headed, the remaining options in the future to get there, and hence what trades have been accomplished in the past to establish what trades are needed now. Classic work established the generic impossibility of efficient yet decentralized monetary exchange. Knowledge of identities of agents, histories of trade and payments, and initial excess demands are needed for implementation, not simply pairwise knowledge of those contemporaneously matched but also information from others with whom contemporaneously matched payment parties have not been matched previously, so they could not know the history in that way. Likewise, there are potential crashes with cryptocurrencies and digital assets. As with circulating private debt as a medium of exchange, mismatch is likely as too much or too little debt is issued. Clearly, there could be problems in using distributed ledgers to keep track of all the information. An encouraging aspect of the featured examples is that there are only key instances that require public information on trade, not entire histories of everyone.

Chapter 11 considers cryptocurrency with an expanded discussion of the role and value of tokens in economies with distributed ledger systems. There are various types of money in existence, some fiat, some backed, as well as credit objects. The standard definitions measure "moneyness" via velocity and frequency of use in payments. In practice, in any given economy, one notes the prevalence of multiple media of exchange. Mechanism design theory pinpoints the special role of tokens relative to fiat money; an unrestricted use of fiat money along the time line of contract implementation can hurt the ability to achieve a constrained optimum. From monetary theory, the value of money can be endogenous, as displayed in various distinct models, depending on who meets whom when. In these models the fundamental welfare theorems fail. Competitive equilibria without money are not Pareto optimal, but money as an intrinsically useless device has value. There is an associated empirical literature that examines whether these bubbles are large enough. Typically, however, there are multiple equilibria, a kind of indeterminacy in value, intrinsic to monetary theory. In other environments money is not needed when market structure is closer to being complete. Still, money can have a value because of its required use to pay taxes or legal stipulations—that is, media of exchange by fiat. Likewise, tokens in hybrid systems can play a role and have value on top of the fiat structures. Indeterminacy of token values in these contexts has remedies in the same roots of monetary theory: real interest and use requirements as with utility coins, both implemented with smart contracts. Tokens can have value via backing, potentially, and we critically review various types of stable coins. An algorithmic digital reserve system with commitment can implement optimal activist token policies armed with transactions data from the distributed ledger.

Chapter 12 offers a partial summary while focusing on major conclusions. An online appendix (which can be found at http://www.robertmtownsend.net/research/online-appendix) provides easy access to some of the key papers in the economics literature and thus details of the models or empirical work, with clickable links.

# 2
# Economies, Obstacles, Welfare, and Measurement

The term *economy* here does not refer exclusively to nation-states. It means villages or towns as communities, regions within a country, and international, cross-country economies. We are not shy about starting with villages as small, open economies in a developing country, then moving to interregional and international money transfers, for example. Of great interest to this conversation are the economies of developing countries that typically have limited financial infrastructure. This is a useful context in which to think about innovation and regulation because in some cases much is known from research about the underlying environment and its current institutions and markets. But these are quite limited on the formal side. Such emerging-market economies also provide useful step-back contexts in which to think about the advantages of various possible versions of DLT for those more familiar with heavily banked economies. There is much that needs to be done in developing countries, where the potential for welfare gains is large and significant. However, as is already apparent, innovation is going on in developed economies, too, where gaps also remain, and those cases are also featured.

## 2.1 Economy

An economy consists of the commodity space, preferences of agents, endowments, and technology. The meaning of the term *agents* depends on the context and applications: households, farms, micro and small businesses, and larger nonfinancial and financial firms, including money-transfer organizations. Each agent has endowments of goods and/or factors of production, preferences in the form of utility functions over goods or profits, and access to technology. Agents can be individuals in a family, households in a village, or firms. Agents can be separated in space, across villages and regions, or traveling about. Key features of an economic environment include time, as in dynamic decision problems, uncertainty and realization of states of the world, and location. An economy is conceptualized in a sufficiently general way so that all the examples above and those in the text below apply.

How should an economy function? Ideally, economies should achieve solutions to programming problems that determine Pareto optimal allocations: an allocation of resources such that one cannot make any one agent or type of agents better off without harming others. Incorporated as well into the programming problem are additional constraints—not simply budget or resource constraints, but constraints that lead to a determination of constrained-optimal allocations: limited information, limited commitment, transaction costs. Alternatively, exogenously imposed contacts can be imposed as realistic, in some settings. More generally, obstacles can vary depending on groups and matches—for example, weak or nonexistent constraints locally in a village but binding constraints among strangers. Money can play a role, as trades are limited among strangers, and money allows such trade—for example, as a communication device displaying past history.

But money can coexist with contracts and other mechanisms or arrangements for those with enduring relationships. Constraints can also vary over time.

The commonality of this framework deserves emphasis. One can think of households running small and medium-sized enterprises (SMEs) interacting with each other in a village in some kind of financial-information regime. Agents in this example are SMEs with capital, labor, and consumption. One can include households that provide wage labor, and in both cases not all transactions need be within the village: Firms purchase inputs and sell products as imports and exports. Furthermore, the same notation applies equally well to groups of financial firms with balance sheets and dividends interacting with each other, such as money-transfer organizations in different countries or broker-dealers in New York financial markets, acting on behalf of clients or on their own account, in the context of larger markets.

In all cases the time line of what happens when is crucial: a specification of unobserved, underlying states; messages among the parties; and multiple actions at potentially different points in time. A recurring focus is what the multiparty arrangements look like currently and whether they are constrained optimal or not.

An example of such a time line is given in figure 2.1.

In addition to contemporary examples of economies, one can go back in time. Economic history makes clear the importance of even rudimentary technologies. Furthermore, when technology changed, so also did economic and financial organizations (Townsend 1990). To highlight one feature, agents can send messages to one another, and the technology for doing this has changed over time, anticipating the discussion of distributed ledgers.

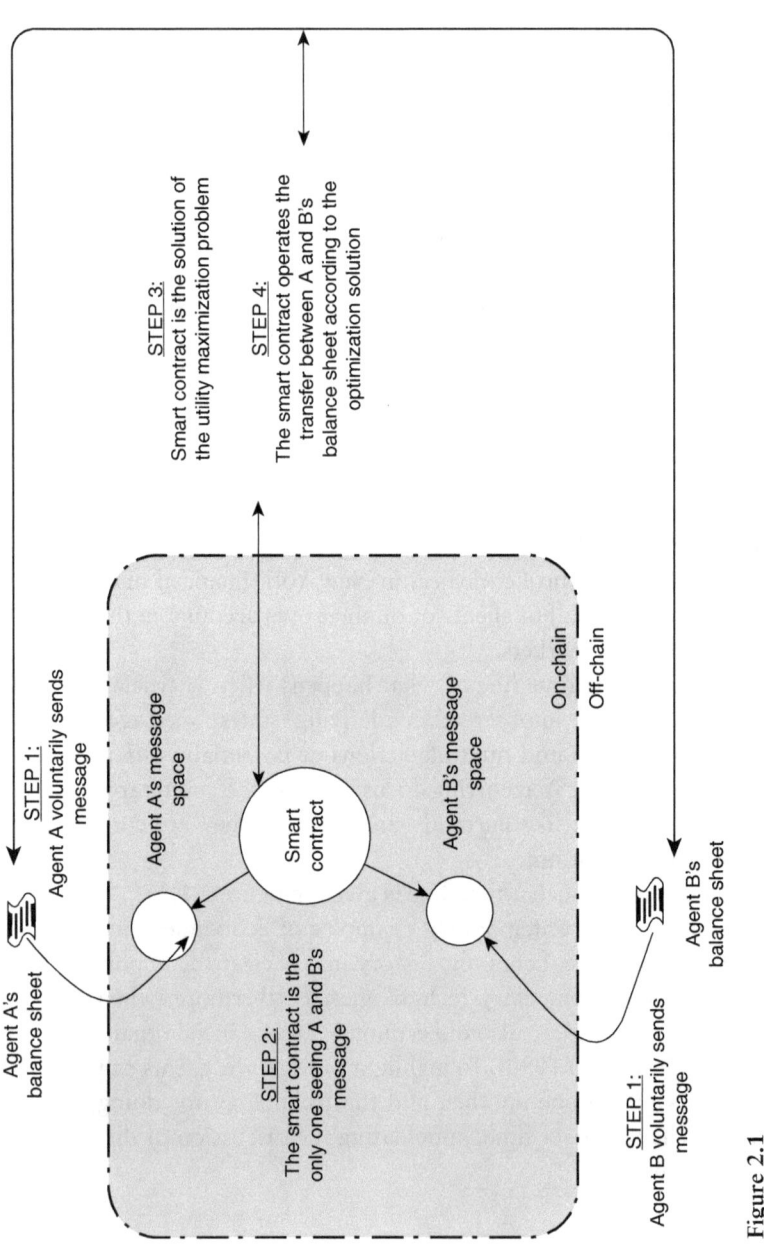

**Figure 2.1**
Schemata of financial accounts and agent interaction through smart contract. Agents A and B with financial accounts are sending messages from an a priori message space; these messages are input into a designed smart contract and execute a transfer that alters the financial accounts. *Source:* Nicolas Zhang (2019).

## 2.2 Measurement

Hand in hand with the conceptualization and presentation of economies come issues of measurement. The standard framework for measurement of economic activity takes the form of integrated financial accounts: the income statement, balance sheet and its change, and the statement of cash flow. This applies for all actors in the economy, households, financial and nonfinancial firms, broker-dealers, government, the standard sectors of the national income and product accounts, and on occasion, more detailed and alternative breakdowns. We may have all these data in some instances for a given economy, as in integrated regional financial accounts, but obviously not always. Sometimes available measurements are sparse. Nevertheless, integrated financial accounts remain the premier organizing principle for economic data.

Bear in mind the obvious: The ledgers of distributed ledgers are a database. Indeed, we present a schematic that we return to below: two agents, $A$ and $B$, each with financial accounts interacting with each other through a smart contract, in effect creating yet more data that can be put on ledgers. We shall explain more subsequently, below, regarding messages, smart contacts, on-chain and off-chain concepts.

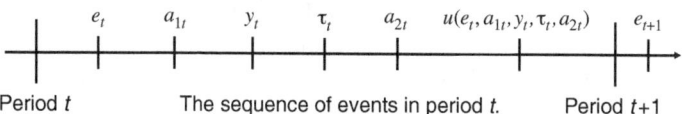

**Figure 2.2**
Illustrative time line of events within a given period $t$ under a contract. The agent observes its current underlying state, $e_t$, then takes an action $a_{1t}$, determining publicly observed state $y_t$, which in turn activates transfer $\tau_t$. Then, toward the end of the period, the agent takes another action, $a_{2t}$, resulting in utility as a function of these actions and events $U(e_t, a_{1t}, y_t, \tau_t, a_{2t})$. At date $t+1$, the state $e_{t+1}$ is realized (determined in part by previous actions) and the time line of $t$ repeats at $t+1$, and so on.
*Source:* Doepke and Townsend (2006).

Figure 2.2 is an example featuring the time line under a particular contact written between two parties, and again we come back to such time lines in subsequent sections. The point here is that ledgers and contracts need to be understood in the context of the underlying economy and its measurement.

## 2.3  Townsend Thai Project

One featured context that appears at various points through this book are the surveyed areas of the Townsend Thai project and the associated database.

An initial, baseline survey conducted in 1997 included villages from four provinces: two in the relatively poor agrarian northeast and two in the developed central region near Bangkok. Within each of these four provinces we chose 12 *tambons* (subcounties) per province. Four villages per tambon were selected randomly. Within each village, households were selected at random from rosters held by the headman. The 1997 household survey has 15 households for each of 192 villages, or 2,880 households. There are also survey instruments for the 192 headmen, 161 preexisting village-level institutions, and 1,920 sets of soil samples.

The baseline survey and data collection were done in April/May of 1997 for rural areas. With the unanticipated Thai financial crisis emerging in July 1997, we began in 1998 the first of many subsequent rural annual resurveys in four randomly chosen tambons in each of the original four provinces. An additional tambon per province was selected for fielding an intensive monthly survey, starting in August of that year.

The scale of the survey expanded: Two more provinces were added in the south in 2003 and two more in the north in 2004, though one province was dropped in each region for insurgency or budgetary reasons. An urban baseline and subsequent annual urban resurvey were added beginning in 2005 to compare urban neighborhoods to rural villages within the same sampled provinces.

The final rounds of data collection gave us 20 years of annual rural surveys, from 1997 to 2017; 11 years of annual urban surveys, from 2005 to 2015; and 231 months of rural monthly surveys. Additional monthly urban data were gathered for 45 months in total. The rural and urban monthly data have been used to create complete financial accounts. The Townsend Thai project data, including these accounts, have been used to measure and analyze financial access, thus making the obvious connection to the social implications of distributed ledgers, as better understanding of what is happening on the ground allows beneficial innovation.

# 3
# Ledgers as Financial Accounts

Here we focus on the most obvious component of distributed ledger technology, namely, the ledgers themselves. The unique advantage of DLT as a ledger is that it can be held in common and shared. As a corollary, DLT provides an additional accounting check beyond double-entry bookkeeping on the reliability of recorded transactions. Furthermore, links of DLT ledgers to financial accounts open up a vision for future innovations that could have great power.

**3.1 Statement of Cash Flow and Balance Sheet as a Ledger: From Paper Currency to Distributed Ledgers in a Few Steps**

We make the link immediately to standard accounting concepts. Cash and paper currency transactions can be recorded on ledgers. For village economies measured in the Townsend Thai project, this is done as in Samphantharak and Townsend (2009), where the statement of cash flow as a standard corporate account is created, along with the stocks recorded in the balance sheet. Tables 3.1, 3.2, and 3.3 provide examples, including the income statement as well.

More specifically, a transaction log operates on the Townsend Thai monthly survey data (http://townsend-thai.mit.edu) and records cash transactions that each household $i$ has with any

**Table 3.1**
Comprehensive financial accounts: balance sheet of household A.

Assets, liabilities, and net worth for a featured household over months 5 through 9

| Month | 5 | 6 | 7 | 8 | 9 |
|---|---|---|---|---|---|
| Cash in hand | 1,966,139 | 1,862,121 | 1,701,863 | 1,663,257 | 1,593,938 |
| Account receivables | 688,971 | 805,259 | 952,359 | 1,059,382 | 1,126,773 |
| Deposits at financial institutions | 167,271 | 167,969 | 168,094 | 156,799 | 157,474 |
| ROSCA (net position) | 33,000 | 37,000 | 41,000 | 11,500 | 16,050 |
| Other lending | 153,136 | 153,136 | 153,136 | 153,136 | 153,136 |
| Inventories | 1,346,939 | 1,440,729 | 1,576,481 | 1,697,413 | 1,842,527 |
| Livestock | 326,280 | 323,018 | 319,787 | 316,590 | 313,424 |
| Fixed assets | 967,342 | 973,759 | 970,949 | 968,151 | 965,365 |
|   Household assets | 598,758 | 596,261 | 593,775 | 591,299 | 588,833 |
|   Agricultural assets | 66,104 | 65,829 | 65,554 | 65,281 | 65,009 |
|   Business assets | 2,479 | 11,669 | 11,620 | 11,572 | 11,523 |
|   Land and other fixed assets | 300,000 | 300,000 | 300,000 | 300,000 | 300,000 |
| **Total assets** | **5,649,079** | **5,762,991** | **5,883,669** | **6,026,228** | **6,168,687** |
| Total liabilities | 1,132,310 | 1,280,270 | 1,425,465 | 1,570,660 | 1,715,855 |
|   Account payables | 1,078,505 | 1,228,465 | 1,375,660 | 1,522,855 | 1,670,050 |
|   Other borrowing | 53,805 | 51,805 | 49,805 | 47,805 | 45,805 |

*(continued)*

**Table 3.1** (continued)

| Month | 5 | 6 | 7 | 8 | 9 |
|---|---|---|---|---|---|
| Total wealth | 4,516,769 | 4,482,721 | 4,458,204 | 4,455,568 | 4,452,832 |
| Initial wealth | 3,439,250 | 3,439,250 | 3,439,250 | 3,439,250 | 3,439,250 |
| Cumulative net gifts received | −6,664 | −6,046 | −6,357 | −6,319 | −7,576 |
| Cumulative savings | 1,084,182 | 1,049,517 | 1,025,311 | 1,022,637 | 1,021,158 |
| **Total liabilities and wealth** | **5,649,079** | **5,762,991** | **5,883,669** | **6,026,228** | **6,168,687** |

The unit of currency is THB. Month 5 is corresponding to January 1999.
*Source:* Samphantharak and Townsend (2009).

**Table 3.2**
Comprehensive financial accounts: income statement of household A.

Revenue, expenses, net profits, and disposition into consumption and savings

| Month | 5 | 6 | 7 | 8 | 9 |
|---|---|---|---|---|---|
| Revenue from cultivation | | | | | |
| Revenue from livestock | 30,485 | 27,753 | 26,180 | 21,780 | 26,730 |
| Livestock produce | 28,985 | 27,753 | 26,180 | 21,780 | 26,730 |
| Capital gains | 1,500 | | | | |
| Revenue from fish and shrimp | | | | | |
| Revenue from business | 184,360 | 145,360 | 183,875 | 152,890 | 160,455 |
| Revenue from labor provision | 11,440 | 11,440 | 11,440 | 11,440 | 11,440 |
| Other revenues | 6,000 | 3,000 | 6,000 | 6,000 | 6,000 |
| **Total revenues** | **232,285** | **187,553** | **227,495** | **192,110** | **204,625** |

*(continued)*

**Table 3.2** (continued)

| Month | 5 | 6 | 7 | 8 | 9 |
| --- | --- | --- | --- | --- | --- |
| Cost of cultivation | | | | | |
| Cost of livestock | 31,944 | 30,281 | 27,642 | 22,813 | 21,715 |
|   Capital losses | | | | | |
|   Depreciation (aging) | 3,281 | 3,263 | 3,230 | 3,198 | 3,166 |
|   Other expenses | 28,663 | 27,018 | 24,412 | 19,615 | 18,549 |
| Cost of fish and shrimp | | | | | |
| Cost of business | 220,176 | 167,323 | 199,933 | 150,300 | 159,472 |
| Cost of labor provision | | | | | |
| Cost of other production activities | | | | | |
| **Total cost of production** | **252,120** | **197,604** | **227,575** | **173,112** | **181,187** |
| Interest revenue | | | | | |
| Interest expense | 55 | 55 | 55 | 75 | 55 |
| Other expenses | 2,794 | 2,783 | 2,810 | 2,798 | 2,786 |
|   Depreciation of fixed assets | 2,794 | 2,783 | 2,810 | 2,798 | 2,786 |
|   Insurance premium | | | | | |
| Extraordinary items | | | | | |
|   Capital gains | | | | | |
|   Capital losses | | | | | |
| **Net income** | **−22,684** | **−12,889** | **−2,945** | **16,125** | **20,597** |
| Consumption | 9,035 | 9,362 | 8,145 | 10,849 | 8,566 |
| Savings | −31,719 | −22,251 | −11,090 | 5,276 | 12,031 |

*Source:* Samphantharak and Townsend (2009).

## Table 3.3
Comprehensive financial accounts: statement of cash flow of household A.

Adjustments to get to cash flow as distinct from accrued income, then cash flow from production, consumption, and financing activities

| Month | 5 | 6 | 7 | 8 |
|---|---|---|---|---|
| Net income (+) | −22,684 | −12,889 | −2,945 | 16,125 |
| Adjustments | | | | |
| Depreciation (+) | 6,075 | 6,046 | 6,040 | 5,996 |
| Change in account receivable (−) | −147,488 | −116,288 | −147,100 | −107,023 |
| Change in account payable (+) | 149,960 | 149,960 | 147,195 | 147,195 |
| Change in inventory (−) | −126,465 | −106,205 | −148,866 | −128,883 |
| Change in other current assets (−) | 1,781 | 3,263 | 3,230 | 3,198 |
| Consumption of household-produced outputs (−) | −350 | −314 | −383 | −373 |
| **Cash flow from production** | −139,171 | −76,427 | −142,830 | −63,765 |
| Consumption expenditure (−) | −8,685 | −9,048 | −7,762 | −10,476 |
| Capital expenditure (−) | −3,281 | −12,463 | −3,230 | −3,198 |
| **Cash flow from consumption and investment** | −11,966 | −21,511 | −10,992 | −13,674 |
| Change in deposit at financial institution (−) | −8,895 | −698 | −125 | 11,295 |
| Change in ROSCA position (−) | −4,000 | −4,000 | −4,000 | 29,500 |
| Lending (−) | 0 | 0 | 0 | 0 |
| Borrowing (+) | −2,000 | −2,000 | −2,000 | −2,000 |
| Net gifts received (+) | −710 | 618 | −311 | 38 |
| **Cash flow from financing** | −15,605 | −6,080 | −6,436 | 38,833 |
| Change in cash holding (from statement of cash flows) | −166,742 | −104,019 | −160,258 | −38,606 |
| Change in cash holding (from balance sheet) | −166,742 | −104,019 | −160,258 | −38,606 |

*Source:* Samphantharak and Townsend (2009).

other household $j$. As with Bitcoin, there is an initial state, that is, who holds coins, as in the balance sheet, a state that is modified by a transaction in the cash flow statement to deliver a new state. A difference with paper currency, though, is that currency is held by the household as part of its balance sheet and is not public. Currency is an actual portable physical token but not an electronic entry. It is very much a decentralized way of keeping track of histories, a point we return to subsequently. But the accounting concepts underlying the use of currency and the use of coins are exactly the same: cash flow and balance sheet.

A formal statement of cash flow goes a bit further. It distinguishes the purpose of the cash outflow (or inflow) and thus records cash used for consumption and investment, for production, and for financing as in borrowing and lending. The households in the Thai villages do not keep these cash flow accounts. However, we constructed one for each surveyed household from the Townsend Thai data. Such cash flow statements are essential for the study of liquidity, hinting at a data use for DLT that we revisit throughout this book. Recording liquidity is an essential feature of many distributed ledger systems and a key aspect of mechanism design.

We can now link the statement of cash flow to the new language of distributed ledgers with only a few conceptual steps, as it is not difficult to imagine how the new technology could map onto the current paper currency systems. First, one could imagine in principle that accounts could be kept on a common account or centralized common ledger. To establish a proof of concept, this is being done with the Townsend Thai data. It is "just" a new integrated database that we are creating. A key step here is whether the transactions that would be recorded on the ledger are consistent with each other, which involves rechecking the database to quantify discrepancies. If $i$ transacts with $j$, is $j$ in the database and, if so, is $j$ also reporting a transaction with $i$? Yet this uncovers discrepancies, and this is one of the main things DLT can remedy. Some of these discrepancies could be innocent measurement errors or honest mistakes in reporting. Unfortunately, when we were first gathering these data two decades years ago, we did not have the conceptualization of the common ledger as a check on the gathered monthly data. These and other types of discrepancies matter, for example, as in the New York financial markets. One purpose of the common ledger component of DLT is to have consensus and avoid subsequent validation.

As an example one can think about Digital Asset's construction for the Australian Stock Exchange (Martin, Lee, and Townsend 2017). First, two parties $A$ and $B$ meet on an outside trading platform and agree to trade. The trade information is sent by the trading platform to the clearing exchange, CSD. The CSD writes an encoded message on the distributed ledgers. The message can be read by $A$ and $B$ and references a contract ID. $A$ and $B$ can read from the distributed ledger the messages that pertain to them and can run Digital Asset's DAML code on the contract to verify that it does what it is expected to do. The contract information makes it into their own personal contract stores. Thus the state of the world, the trade in this instance, is recorded by consensus on a shared distributed ledger. We shall return to the encryption aspects of such transactions in a subsequent section.

In the Thai context, the distributed ledgers could also be implemented in practice—in real time—if transactions were out of e-wallet coins and hence recorded (electronic measurement more generally comes up in the next section). Next, the common ledger could be created and distributed among the households so that each has access to the common account or to its own identical copy (subject to privacy, which we come back to under mechanism design in chapter 6). We would call this new common integrated database a *distributed ledger*.

In summary, the idea of ledgers as a statement of cash flow is not at all new. Yet when put on a common database, discrepancies can be readily spotted and corrected. Approved histories can be thought of as immutable. A limitation is that only subsets of transactions might be recorded, in which case coordinated statements of cash flow could be incomplete. On the other hand, the vision for further utility comes with the creation of complete and integrated accounts.

## 3.2 Financial Accounts as Ledgers More Generally

A unified, more comprehensive measurement of the financial environment is represented by the entire set of complete financial accounts. Specifically, measured transactions can be used to create formal financial statements, not only the statement of cash flow and balance sheet but also the income statement. More specifically, one can use an initial baseline survey to enumerate financial and real assets held at the beginning point in the time line of the survey.[1] Items on the balance sheet would be the amount of currency held, land, and other assets. Indeed, when on a common ledger, this links to the idea in cryptography of using ledgers as a registry of secure property titles. Likewise, cryptocurrency on the balance sheet would be an asset, hence termed a *digital asset*.

Of course, liabilities can be measured in the same way. Subtraction of liabilities from assets thus determines initial net worth. Then there are transactions over time. A household, for example, surrenders currency to buy another asset. Currency can be used to buy consumption, an expense on the income statement, and income is received as revenue on the income statement. The difference in revenues and expenses is saving, which, along with incoming gifts and remittances, must be equivalent with an increase in net assets. The statement of cash flow is similar to the income statement except that for the income statement, one typically uses an accrued income concept. Expenses are booked only when there is revenue, as in finance, to measure profits as the return on assets used to operate projects. The distinction between accrual and cash flow methods allows for the distinction between productivity and liquidity and is often essential.

A key point to note is that a given transaction in the data can and typically will enter multiple times across individual statements. Thus, the changes in balance sheet and income statement must be consistent with each other. The books have to balance. This is the idea behind double-entry bookkeeping, done for accuracy at the individual entity level, which was a huge innovation at the time the concept was invented. Luca Pacioli, whose work was published in 1494, is considered to be the "father of accounting," but the inventor could have been Benedetto Cotrugli, even earlier, in 1458. The use of distributed and common ledgers to reduce discrepancies is another layer on top of the conventional double-entry account and is arguably as important an innovation as double-entry bookkeeping.[2] This is a more accurate system than accounts individually. All this comes from the log of transactions.

Of course, to create the complete financial accounts from a distributed ledger, certain metadata have to be recorded as part of measured transactions. Again, as an example, the code that creates the accounts for the Townsend Thai data operates on the underlying transactions data, preprogrammed to recognize, from the questions to which the transaction answers are given, where in the accounts particular transactions should be entered. Any entity (e.g., a large firm) is doing this with its own proprietary financial accounts, so the firm at least knows the nature of its own transactions through the lens of financial accounts. In contrast, a distributed ledger that records only transactions without categorization cannot be used to create complete financial accounts. The middle common ground is perhaps the most interesting: Transacting parties record the categorization, and reconciliation seeks to make the categorization common. This could be an additional advance made possible with common ledgers: *consensus categorization*. The common accounts component of DLT could allow this to be done while maintaining privacy, just as DLT can remove discrepancies in trade.

To sum up, complete financial accounts can have value for the accuracy of measurement, for analysis of data, and hence for the households and businesses themselves. The log of transactions can have value for policy.

We now turn to two example applications that convey the value of enhanced financial accounts for policy in emerging markets and in the United States, to track the impact of tariffs or liberalizations and to measure liquidity flows to build microfounded macro models. A subsequent section on cryptocurrency shows how a log of transactions can be used specifically as a basis for an activist cryptocurrency policy of a digital reserve bank.

## 3.3 Two Examples of the Use of Village and Community-level Financial Accounts: Tariffs vs. Real and Financial Liberalization and Liquidity Accounts for Multiple Media of Exchange

There is huge interest in the impact of tariffs in the United States, under the Trump administration, and it would be useful for trade and financial flows to be recorded in real time. Likewise, in reverse, one could examine the impact of trade and financial liberalizations in emerging markets.

Paweenawat and Townsend (2012) follow the Bureau of Economic Analysis (2017) guidelines and show first how to reconfigure household and business financial statements and, second, how to aggregate up to create the set of national income and product accounts (NIPA), with the economy as the village. The income statement is transformed, being careful about value added to the production account, and the balance sheet is transformed by taking time differences to create the savings/investment account. Flow of funds accounts measure net acquisition of financial assets, assets minus net incurrence of liabilities, which is equivalent to gross savings less expenditures on real capital. The balance-of-payments account of the village economy follows, thus explaining how villages, and regions, interact with each other.

## 3.4 A Counterfactual Policy Analysis

Paweenawat and Townsend (2018) calibrate a model that integrates real and financial sectors, allowing for occupation choice, trade in goods across manufacturing and agricultural sectors, and external borrowing and lending. The model has judiciously chosen obstacles to trade—namely, transactions costs for commodity trade and collateral requirements for credit. After fitting the model-generated village paths to the data, one can examine simultaneously and consistently the activities of the featured case study of sampled households and businesses along with selected aggregates. That is, one can determine what is happening over time at the household level with their own financial accounts and what is happening at the economy-wide, village level with the NIPA accounts. One can also distinguish movements of real capital from movements in paper currency.

It then becomes possible to conduct counterfactual policy analysis: What if trade and capital flows had not been allowed to liberalize, or alternatively, what would happen if there were further innovations stemming from an enhanced financial infrastructure? If, for example, there had been a push for protection in the past, and somehow trade across regions had been more restricted, then a wedge would move relative prices. Likewise, one can examine counterfactual restrictions on interregional flows of capital if more savings had been targeted to be invested at home. The model predicts what would have happened to interest rates, wages, and prices; to occupation choice, production, profits, and earnings; and, finally, to the trade balance, the current account, and the balancing flows of borrowing/lending.

The impact of altered policy is not homogeneous. Removing an obstacle at the village level, through DLT or other means, is not the same thing as increasing social value. Likewise, imposing obstacles can be welfare improving for some households as a function of balance sheets and income flows.[3] The application is, of course, not specific to Thailand. One can imagine examining the impacts of tariffs and flows of funds in the US, if we were to have the requisite data.

### 3.5 Generalized Statements of Liquidity Accounts in the US

Nothing in these examples is particular to Thailand and the predominant use of paper currency as the medium of exchange there. Samphantharak, Schuh, and Townsend (2016) show how a conventional statement of cash flows can be made for advanced countries such as the United States. Using actual data, the statement of cash flow for households is disaggregated into item-by-item liquidity accounts: the inflows and outflows to and from demand deposits; credit, debit, and prepaid cards; and paper currency. Likewise, though not yet well measured in the surveys of the Federal Reserve Bank of Boston, the statement of liquidity accounts links conceptually to the other financial accounts and thus to the variation in income and long-term financial assets.

Of course, distributed ledger technology is not yet the source of data, though one can envision how we might get there. The Boston Fed survey uses data from survey questionnaires and data from diaries. Likewise, data from the Survey of Consumer Finances (SCF) and Panel Study of Income Dynamics (PSID) are interview-based. Still, there is increasing use of administrative data (which is electronic) as a cross-check on consumer responses. For example: Are households reporting bank transactions consistent with data from corresponding banks? Browning, Crossley, and Winter (2014) seek to integrate the collection of wealth, income, and spending data in the British Household Panel Survey so that for each household the intertemporal budget constraint holds. An Office for National Statistics (ONS) Economic Expert Working Group (EEWG) envisions using web surveys, mobile surveys, and phone apps to scan barcodes and till receipts. There is now also electronic data surrendered voluntarily by customers, as with Mint, and the use of commercial bank information by information aggregators. Use of DLT to create complete financial accounts is not as far as away as it might seem, *a priori*.

How could this data be used? As emphasized here in this section, we could see and understand better the role of liquidity in an economy. Work emphasizing liquidity and payments and links to monetary policy is a bit sparse but increasing. Significant recent contributions include Kaplan and Violante (2014), Piazzesi and Schneider (2018), Adrian and Shin (2009), Doepke and Schneider (2006), Auclert (2019), and Fulford and Schuh (2017). DLT creates the capability of providing enhanced measurement over and above current US surveys. Currently there are discrepancies between the cash flows associated with aggregated income statements and the cash flows associated with changes in aggregated balance sheets (Samphantharak, Schuh, and Townsend 2016).

## 3.6 DLT vs. Traditional Database: Limitations of Distributed Databases to Be Recognized and Incorporated in Designs

A ledger could be viewed as a traditional database in which a user can create, read, update, or delete (CRUD) (Ray 2017). The risk in having centralized control of a database is that anyone with sufficient access to it can destroy or corrupt data, so users are reliant on the security infrastructure of the database operator and must trust those with write capabilities. The March 2019 episode with Capital One and the Amazon Cloud, hacked by a former employee, is illustrative.

In contrast, distributed ledgers use decentralized data storage, in the sense that the ledgers are distributed among users. With cryptographic rules for change, security is inherent in this structure; there is no single copy. With distributed ledgers a user can read and retrieve data—that is, audit records—and a user can write by adding more data to append only. Newly proposed transactions must be validated in some way, as is discussed in chapter 5. Likewise, past validated histories are immutable. There is no updating of past transactions and no deletion. A key property of blockchains such as Bitcoin is that they do not rely on a single trusted third party as trustee or notary to intermediate transactions. The blockchain network enforces execution, giving this a social aspect. This is what Nakamoto (2008) meant by a system without a trusted third party.

But with the decentralized system of distributed ledgers comes known database problems (Wikipedia 2019a). A theorem in computer science, the CAP theorem, states that it is impossible for a distributed data store to simultaneously provide more than two out of the following three guarantees: (i) Consistency—where every read receives the most recent write or an error; (ii) Availability—where every request receives a (nonerror) response, without the guarantee that it contains the most recent write as with consistency; (iii) Partition tolerance—in which the system continues to operate despite an arbitrary number of messages being dropped (or delayed) by the network between nodes, so that there is a partition, multiple versions.

To highlight further, in the presence of allowing partitions, one has to choose between consistency and availability. That is, when a network partition occurs, one has to decide to cancel the operation, which decreases availability but ensures consistency, or proceed with the operation but risk inconsistency.

Furthermore, even when the system is running normally, there is a tension between consistency and availability because of latency. Latency is the amount of time a message takes to traverse a system, or how much time it takes for a packet of data to get from one designated point to another (Wikipedia 2018b). High-speed but virtually instantaneously available systems run into latency issues, as this can create inconsistency across multiple versions. With Corda, for example, latency determines the geographic distribution of validators, in some instances, to mitigate delay.

More specifically, we come to the Fischer Consensus Problem of distributed computing (Fischer, Lynch, and Paterson 1985), though we need some definitions first:

> In computer science, synchronization refers to one of two distinct but related concepts: synchronization of processes, and synchronization of data. Process synchronization refers to the idea that multiple processes are to join up or handshake at a certain point, in order to reach an agreement or commit to a certain sequence of action. Data synchronization refers to the idea of keeping multiple copies of a dataset in coherence with one another, or to maintain data integrity. Process synchronization primitives are commonly used to implement data synchronization. (Wikipedia 2019b)

Otherwise the process is asynchronous.

Fischer proved that it is impossible to guarantee that any asynchronously connected set of communicating nodes can agree on even a single bit value—a devastating result. On the other hand, the Fischer consensus problem can be resolved simply by synchronizing from a single point. However, doing so introduces a single point of centralization, which is ironic given the decentralized connotation of DLT as emphasized in chapter 1. This centralization in turn can cause scaling problems—that is, as in many DLT consensus algorithms, every node must be connected to every other to achieve consensus, and the costs of messages rise exponentially with the number of nodes. Computer science/distributed systems bounce between these problems: CAP in asynchronous systems, and scaling and fault tolerance in synchronous systems. These features should drive choices as part of a constrained-optimal design (Mallett 2019).

Again, the various distinct consensus protocols for validation cope with these problems in alternative ways and illustrate the trade-off between hyped decentralization, which has high congestion because of the underlying centralized features, and named validators, including single validator systems, which again raises the issue of trusted third parties. The existence of a trusted third party can greatly enhance speed and lower costs. Another example is Digital Asset's innovation for the Australian stock exchange. Adopting the language of Casey et al. (2018), these systems are known as "permissioned" (or "private") blockchains, with a limited set of entities, or even a single organization, allowed to write to the blockchain. This can reduce scaling problems.

Another example highlighted in Casey et al. (2018), the Lightning Network, aims to greatly reduce cost and time constraints by shifting small transactions to a cryptographically secure "off-chain" environment so that only large netting transactions need to be directly settled into a resource-constrained blockchain. With Hyperledger Fabric, a permissioned blockchain, a third-party auditor or regulator can obtain provably correct answers to queries about the system as a whole using zero-knowledge proof concepts. Centralized DLT exchanges for cryptocurrency have "relayers," application interfaces that allow users to trade in a decentralized manner (Bronstein 2018).

Mallett (2009) compares strictly hierarchical/client servers with fully connected mesh networks and then speaks to the advantages of partial mesh networks. The point is to compare and potentially select among network designs. The US military uses a hierarchical system that suffers from a lack of incorporation of local information but minimizes latency by minimizing communication, as one-way commands from headquarters are obeyed. These hybrid designs need to be integrated further with economic systems, and, indeed, the industrial and management organization may be endogenous with the design selected.

As a suggestive example, Townsend (1978) uses simple, transaction-cost arguments, with fixed costs per node for any given bilateral connection. Optimal risk-sharing arrangements partition agents into segregated subgroups. Despite ever-decreasing per capita costs and ever-increasing gains from having all agents in one mutual fund, due to portfolio diversification and the law of large numbers, marginal costs can exceed marginal benefits from increasing group size. More generally, a related economic issue is whether to have over-the-counter (OTC) markets, centralized platforms, or a hybrid in between. Although it may seem advantageous to have all trade taking place in one spot, the transaction costs integrated with economics may suggest otherwise, potentially.

The main conclusion is that there are trade-offs in design. Which system might dominate is a function of the environment and goals.

# 4

# E-Payments, E-Messages, and Trusted Third Parties in Payment Systems

In this chapter we compare and contrast Thailand to Sweden and then put Kenya in between as home of an impressive innovation in e-payments with measured, documented welfare gains. The point is that gains can be large even for mundane systems using components of distributed ledger technology (DLT), gains that remain to be harvested in many low-income and developing countries.

## 4.1 Thailand and the Predominant Use of Paper Currency

In emerging markets, such as those in Southeast Asia, 55% to 90% of all payment transactions are conducted through physical cash payments, fiat money provided by the central bank. The ratio of currency to gross domestic product (GDP) is 11.37 for all of Thailand, the fourth highest among countries listed in a 2015 study (Rogoff 2016). Based on currency and coin outstanding and measurement income and consumption in GDP, Thailand is estimated to have individual per capita currency holdings equal to seven months of consumption, on average. Asian countries have a high ratio of currency to GDP relative to the rest of the world, generally.

Alvarez, Pawasutipaisit, and Townsend (2018) use data that were gathered monthly in the Townsend Thai project,

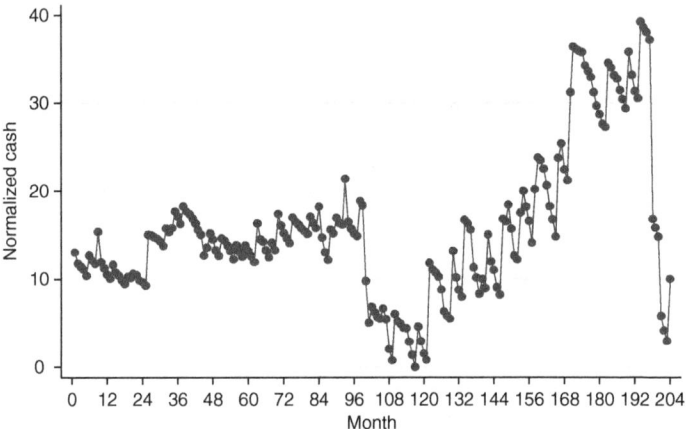

**Figure 4.1**
Illustrative movement of currency balances for a selected household. Erratic but increasing levels of currency over time, with sharp drop at the end.
*Source:* Townsend Thai Project (2019) data.

**Table 4.1**
Money in terms of monthly consumption.

Means, median, quartiles, and standard deviation of currency balances

|       | mean | sd | p25 | p50 | p75 | N |
|-------|------|----|-----|-----|-----|---|
| Total | 45 | 37 | 21 | 32 | 57 | 531 |

*Source:* Townsend Thai Project (2019) data.

with consumption biweekly, in 16 villages. See figure 4.1 and table 4.1.

They find that typical households running small businesses use paper currency for small and large transactions, spending on consumption in normal times, with spikes in unusual times for durable goods and rotating savings and credit association (ROSCA) transactions. They receive paper currency from income in normal times, with spikes coming from land sales, loans, and gifts. The costs of cash mismanagement are calculated to be of the order of magnitude of 2% to 9.5% of monthly consumption. The top end of that range corresponds with fitting the Miller and Orr (1966) model for businesses adding an ingredient, occasional free transactions, as for households in the Alvarez and Lippi (2009) study in Italy. Businesses in the Thai setting are household-run small and medium-sized enterprises (SMEs). The calculation of costs uses an optimized value function from a dynamic program, the minimized discounted present value cost of holding cash. The lower end of the range of costs corresponds with the interest rate on bank accounts multiplied by average cash holdings. Costs are nontrivial even at the low end of the range. This is far higher than estimated costs of business cycles, for example, and does not consider the costs of printing and distributing the currency. There are gains to be had from moving away from paper currency to electronic systems that could allow payment of interest.

## 4.2 Sweden as an Almost Cashless Society

The Riksbank began in the 1980s to make systematic efforts to shift a large part of the cost of managing paper currency to the private sector, so the private sector would internalize cash management. The number of central bank branches was successively reduced, from one in each province to 20 nationally, and now down to one cash distribution center staffed by eight people. Price distortions were corrected as banks were asked to pay transport costs. The Riksbank's role is limited to printing, transportation to the single cash center, and the destruction of defective and obsolete notes and coins. The private sector has coordinated and allowed interoperability: one credit card network for clearing, one single bank ID, and one mobile application (Swish) for low-value payments, with

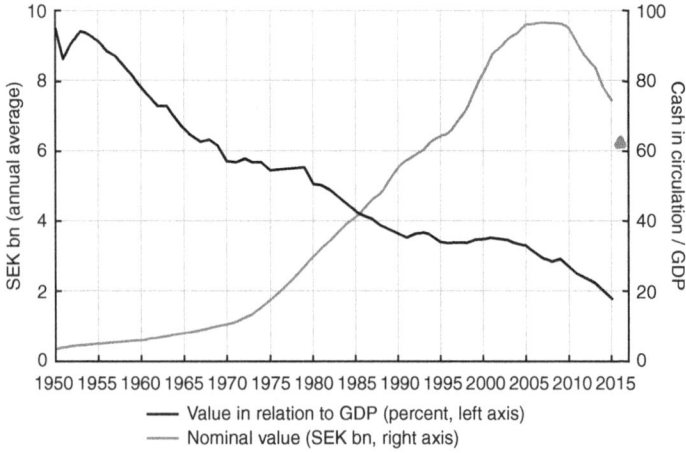

**Figure 4.2**
Swedish currency (SEK) in levels and relative to GDP.
*Source:* Statistics Sweden and Sveriges Riksbank (2018).

the single central bank cash center operating as a decentralized wholesaler between banks and the Riksbank (Ingves 2016; Skingsley 2016).

Sweden is currently down to less than 2.5 as a ratio of paper currency per GDP, one of the lowest in the world (see figure 4.2).

Sweden is a highly digitized country, with most transactions occurring in electronic form under debit cards, credit cards, and e-transfers, as reported in a Sveriges Riksbank survey (2018). Card payments per person are among the highest in the world. There are various electronic clearing systems with financial institutions as key nodes intermediating payments: 160 million transactions yearly in the data-clearing system (owned by the Swedish Bankers' Association); 180 million transactions in the Swish system in 2018; 800 million transactions yearly in the Bankgirot system; and 2.2 billion card payments.[1] Not all of these data are public, but they exist in electronic form, obviously.

## 4.3 Kenya: M-Pesa as an E-Money Innovation with Large Social Gains

Kenya lies midway between currency-intensive Thailand and virtually cashless Sweden. In this context, e-money has had great social value, especially for certain segments of the population. More generally, the potential of new technologies to transform traditional systems is significant. The rate of adoption even among low-income populations is impressive (see figure 4.3).

E-money systems have been endorsed by the Group of Twenty (G20) as an opportunity to build financial markets by constructing new financial systems that increase financial access for large unbanked populations in developing countries (G20 Research Group 2013). Again, the social goal is apparent.

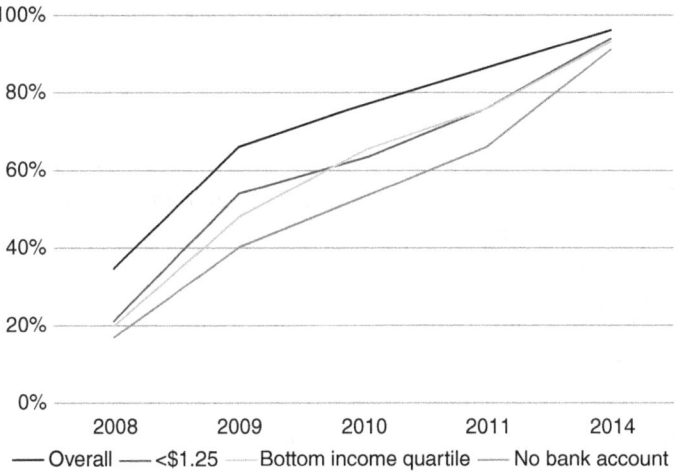

**Figure 4.3**
M-Pesa adoption rates for the entire Kenyan population as well as for the poor, the lowest income quartile, and those with no bank account.
*Source:* Jack and Suri (2014) data.

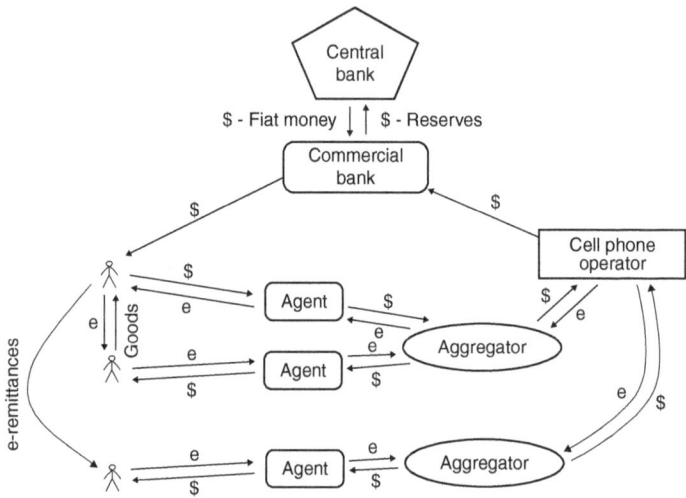

**Figure 4.4**
A schemata of the operational flows of the Kenyan M-Pesa system. An exchange of Kenya shillings, marked as $, for cell phone credits, marked as $e$, with a Safaricom agent; use of this e-money by the customer for purchases or remittances; and a larger picture of the flows of e-money and the cash throughout the system.
*Source:* Jack, Suri, and Townsend (2010).

More specifically, M-Pesa is an e-money implemented by Safaricom (see figure 4.4).

Households can go to a company agent and exchange Kenyan shillings for cell phone credits, which can then be used for purchases or money transfers. For example, a migrant worker in Nairobi can send cell-credits back to relatives in the village, where on request an agent there cashes them back into shillings. This is a functional and comprehensive value transfer system in the context of the actual rugged environment of the economy that gave birth to it.

M-Pesa functions as a "stable coin"—that is, with a fixed local exchange rate to fiat currency. Notably, the exchange between cell accounts and Kenyan shillings is 1–1, apart from a schedule of prespecified transaction costs. These costs are quite low: 6% for tiny values and falling to less than 1% for larger values. This is one-sixth of Western Union's rates and one-twelfth of Postal Pay's rates. In Kenya, Safaricom is a single trusted third party, keeping all of the accounts, though of course customers can see their own accounts and verify that transactions with an agent are happening in real time as requested. The technology uses relatively inexpensive cell phones. Adoption in Kenya among those without bank accounts rose from 20% in 2008 to 90% by 2014.[2]

There is social value to M-Pesa. Studies have shown that M-Pesa aids in economy-wide risk-sharing (Suri 2017). The staggered nature of the rollout allowed a quasi-natural experimental evaluation. Consumption is smoother and more immune from households' specific income shocks. Households are the agents of the general model outlined at the outset. Value can be transferred from households running budget surpluses to those running deficits, for example, and transferred among individual members of a household across regions. Mobile money has also allowed a more efficient allocation of labor and resulted in a meaningful reduction of poverty (Jack and Suri 2014).

Nonbank fintechs such as M-Shwari use M-Pesa to lend to this low-income population, accessing both the record of transactions in a scoring system and using M-Pesa as the payment/repayment medium. There are now over 20 digital credit providers in Kenya.[3] Scoring systems for credit are using the transaction data recorded in M-Pesa.

Yet to be emphasized here, and key to the discussion earlier, Safaricom does not refer to its system as a distributed ledger system. The ledgers are not distributed. They are owned and operated by Safaricom with customers permitted to see individual pieces and make associated approved transactions. Put another way, customers see Safaricom accounts for balances of their ownership of M-Pesa cell-credits and can verify transfers. Customers could but likely do not keep their own accounts of their currency holdings and transactions. Safaricom has complete accounts for cell-credits for all customers and is the trusted third party running that database. It is trusted not to tamper with and to honor requests for redemption of cell-credits back into currency. Likewise, the e-money M-Pesa is not categorized as a cryptocurrency.

This can be fine. In Kenya, it has worked well so far. One does not need to incorporate all the components of DLT in order for the implementation of a subset of components to have value.

One cannot help but note, though, that Safaricom could be tempted to lend its cash funds and thus would look more like a bank, with fractional reserve banking. Actually its funds are put on deposit in commercial banks and the interest is contributed to charity. The advent of M-Pesa and its approval by Kenya's Ministry of Finance was possible precisely because Safaricom is not classified as a commercial bank. Yet in countries such as Kenya, bank runs and failures are commonplace. For this reason, as they and others began to think about these risks, Safaricom switched to depositing its funds into multiple banks. The point: There are limits to trusted third parties, if not direct then indirect. In some contexts, third-party trust is a real issue for individual institutions and for governments.

## 4.4  The Role of Broker-Dealers, Shortages, Thin Markets, and Common Concerns about Liquidity in Various Disparate Contexts

Dealers in private e-money and paper currency face shortages of liquidity of one object or another, and this can show up in various ways. Returning to M-Pesa and the example of Kenya, Jack and Suri (2011) surveyed households that used M-Pesa and the agents that were contractual spatial outposts for Safaricom. As reported in Jack, Suri, and Townsend (2010), agents ran out of one object or the other on a regular basis. Over 60% of agents ran out of e-money anywhere from approximately once a month to multiple times a day. Likewise, close to 50% of dealers ran out of Kenyan shillings. Recall that the exchange is guaranteed to be 1–1 with no variation in prices or transactions fees. Shortages typically occur with fixed prices, of course. In other situations, one might imagine varying prices but with the potentially lingering problems of thin markets (that is, not many participants).

New systems emerge to cope with these challenges. In Kenya, there are transfers and borrowing/lending among Safaricom agents in a kind of informal market, which includes gifts. Interagent markets could be formalized and potentially improved upon, though of course subject to the obstacles of the environment. Here, with costly transport of fiat paper currency, spatial ingredients play an inherent role. While the e-part is virtually instantaneous, paper currency has to get to the agent. No formal system has as yet been designed.

So-called rebalancing is an issue in other developing countries, too. A report by the Helix Institute of Digital Finance (2017) shows that: agents in Indonesia acting on behalf of banks use the nearest bank branch; 51% require more e-float and 23% need cash; and 63% state that they face barriers in managing liquidity, for example, the lack of resources to buy sufficient amounts of cash or float, unpredictable fluctuations in client demand, and time taken to reach the rebalancing point. They want financial support for liquidity management.

In a very different context, in value and location, but quite close conceptually, consider the New York financial market system. There is interbank borrowing and lending of excess reserves and broker-dealers provide liquidity to this market. As documented in Cocco, Gomes, and Martins (2009), the relationships of traders with dealers who have low correlation in liquidity shocks allow insurance against a shortage of funds. Lagos and Zhang (2018) note the role of liquidity in monetary policy.[4] In this sense, the shortages are a driving force. In this New York context, though, unlike the Kenyan example, the market consists entirely of e-objects. Plus, there are continuing innovations; see Li and Schürhoff (2012) and Hendershott and Madhavan (2015). Still, problems remain; there is considerable scope for improvements in the e-infrastructure systems that are used today.

Likewise, functioning cryptocurrency exchange platforms should be integral rather than peripheral to the debate about tokens and distributed ledgers. They function quite differently. Brokers in markets can provide liquidity through implicit insurance but are, potentially, charging usurious markups and committing fraud. The most popular cryptocurrency exchanges, such as Coinbase, Binance, and Kraken, are implemented as centralized exchanges, thus offering an ironic contrast with so-called decentralized coins. These crypto-exchanges rely on traditional technology, where customers can access and trade using e-mail and simple passwords. This is what has led to hacking episodes. However, contemporary decentralized exchanges using DLT technology, which include 0x, Protocol, AirSwap, and OmiseGO, are thought by some to be difficult to use, have limited capability, and display low volume (Glazer 2018).

In conclusion, innovation in financial infrastructure may be possible. On the other hand, there may not be inherent contradictions, as tokens and exchanges fulfill different economic functions: one to provide record of ownership and the other to facilitate exchange. It is an advantage of economic analysis that we can draw these distinctions, getting beneath the hype. A core issue is whether or not new distributed ledger–based trading platforms lower clearly identified costs relative to legacy systems.

# 5
# Encryption

Cryptocurrencies are e-message systems similar in their basics to M-Pesa but differing in the amount of cryptography used, the diverse methods for validation of transactions, and the public nature of the ledgers.

## 5.1  Featured Historical Episodes

One might have thought this cryptography component is what makes DLT new, but that is not the case. The use of cryptography goes back at least to the Mesopotamians, who used it as a key part of their economic and messaging systems. The internet's TCP/IP communications protocol is reminiscent of that, where pieces are put into "envelopes" and encased by beginning and ending bits and then disseminated.

## 5.2  Historical Examples of Encryption

From 7500 to 3500 BC, in Mesopotamia, the code for communication consisted of tokens of some six types and distinct shapes representing particular commodities. Then, around 3500–3100 BC, new complex tokens were covered with lines or dots (figure 5.1a) conferring qualitative and quantitative information (Schmandt-Besserat 2014). Eventually, tokens were put in clay envelopes (figure 5.1b) as a manifest for shipping goods, sealed so that tampering with the manifest would be evident on arrival, as would theft of cargo, as a check of the actual cargo inventory against the manifest would reveal. Writing on the clay manifest envelopes to convey contents of the message (and cargo) is what gave birth to cuneiform writing (Trubek 2015).

If the sender and receiver of the shipment trusted each other, they could be sure there was no tampering by not-trusted parties in between. Better put, any tampering of the invoice or

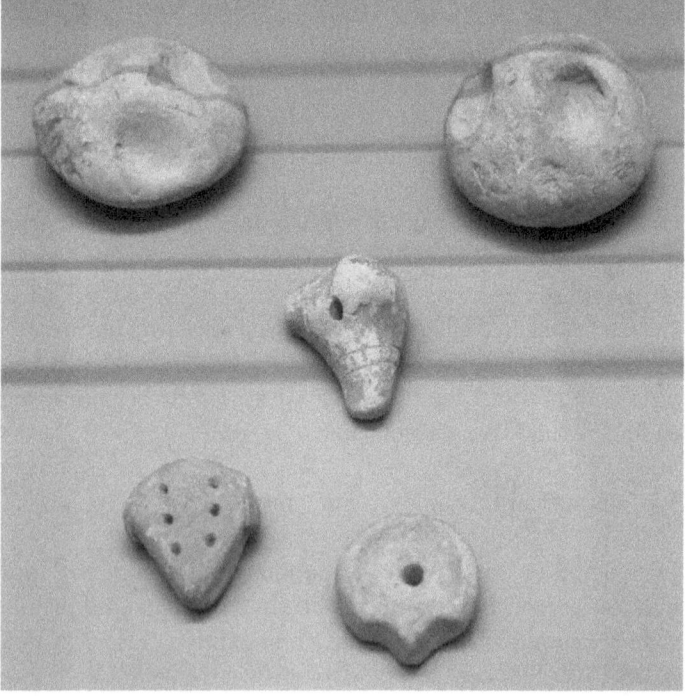

**Figure 5.1a**
Mesopotamia tokens.
*Source:* Wikipedia.

Figure 5.1b

theft of the shipment that took place in between would be self-evident to the receiver. In effect, it was as if the receiver had a code that could unlock the envelope while others in between could not, apart from the sender that created the envelope code in the first place.

Another historical example: Tally sticks as messages and proof of contract emerged as monies in medieval England and were used for centuries, including as a means of payment (Harford 2017). Tallies were a way of recording debts with a system. Willow sticks recorded the original debt transaction and then were split in half (see figure 5.2).

With a distinctive grain, the two halves would match only each other, providing the requisite proof. The lender's half, called the tally stock, was used as a safe and convenient form of payment (hence the word "stock"). When cashed in, the two halves were checked (hence the word "check"). The original borrower paid back the loan to the third-party holder of the asset upon presentation. Here, the original borrower was trusted to repay while the tally stick provided a trustless record of the original promise to lenders and third parties and a record to the borrower that the holder was presenting the

**Figure 5.2**
Medieval English tally sticks.
*Source:* Winchester City Council Museums.

**Figure 5.3**
A decision to burn the obsolete tally sticks in 1834 nearly destroyed the Palace of Westminster.
*Source:* Wikimedia Commons.

original claim (no double presentation of debt). Tally sticks came to an odd conclusion (see figure 5.3).[1]

## 5.3 Contemporary Encryption

This historical discussion leads to key issues in computer science and algorithms. Messages can consist of individual transactions, blocks of transactions, datasets, and other documents. The key to encryption is the one-way function. The underlying message is hashed into a 32-byte (256-bit) message, as in Secure Hash Algorithm SHA-256, and any change at all in the underlying message produces an entirely different hash. One can go from the input data to the hash but not from the hash back to the input data. The hashed output is referred to as a fingerprint. The hash does not reveal the underlying input, and any attempt to tamper produces a different hash, which is easily verified. The underlying message is secure.

A central component is public/private key cryptography. Keys come in pairs—public keys that may be disseminated widely and private keys that are known only to the owner. The generation of such keys depends on cryptographic algorithms based on mathematical problems to produce the one-way functions. Effective security only requires keeping the private key private. In such a system, any person can encrypt a message using the public key, but that encrypted message can only be deciphered with the private key. Roughly, it is known who sent the message but not what the message is. Public key algorithms are fundamental security ingredients ensuring the confidentiality, authenticity, and nonreputability of electronic communications and data storage. They underpin various internet standards.

IBM was installing crypto express cards into its mainframes by 2009. A key distinction now is the perfectly opaque computational systems, which do not allow participants to look inside during computation, versus zero-knowledge proof systems, which do allow participants to look in and find proof that each subset of code ran as intended.

### 5.4 Validation and Distributed Consensus

The roots of distributed ledgers come from distributed consensus, a concept that has been studied for decades in computer science. The traditional application promotes reliability in distributed computing systems. Narayanan et al. (2016) define a distributed consensus protocol as one in which there are $n$ nodes that have an input value. Some of these nodes are faulty or malicious. A distributed consensus protocol has two properties: It must terminate with all honest nodes in agreement on value, and the value must have been generated by honest nodes. This, again, is the basis of secure multiparty computation.

We come to a clear definition of distributed ledgers as multiple, distrusting organizations that run a protocol to create an append-only log in which all participants can verify the integrity of entries appended to the log.[2] This definition has an advantage because it does not refer to trusted third parties; otherwise it is ambiguous whether there is one common trusted party or layers of trust. It is sufficient that there be some distrust.

To set the stage for this discussion, we present the aptly named Byzantine Generals Problem, which has its roots in distributed computing. A subset of a group of generals consists of potential traitors, bad nodes that are either malicious or sending error-ridden messages (Lamport, Shostak, and Pease 1982; Robinson 2009). The decision the generals must make is whether to attack or withdraw—that is, approve transactions or not—and this requires consensus. The generals exchange messages with each other. If the number of potential traitors (faults) is known, and all other nodes tell the truth, then, intuitively, cross-checking a sufficient number of messages is sufficient. However, the degree of difficulty is a function of primitive assumptions. If a coordinator is assumed to always send honest messages, then things are easier, as one only needs to check a small sample of other nodes—a bit of centralization. If the coordinator could be faulty, more cross-checks are needed. If nodes somehow cannot lie about what they have heard, that is helpful, though this requires more rounds. If nodes start repeating what they have heard from others, the group may have to abandon the primary coordinator node.

Here, as an overview, are some of the key differences among existing consensus protocols.[3]

Unlike a bank's or telcom's centralized ledger of account balances, validators in a network must achieve consensus. Bitcoin and Ethereum use proof of work (PoW), in which nodes in a network compete with computing power to solve cryptographic math puzzles and reach consensus. Anyone can do this mining; membership is open, and miners can join and/or leave. Byzantine Fault Toleration (BFT) is actually a property of an algorithm, not the algorithm itself. Sometimes the algorithm is referred to as a Byzantine Agreement. BFT normally means the algorithm is guaranteed to converge or is capable of reaching consensus, even if there are adversarial nodes or if nodes drop from the network. In practical BFT (PBFT) algorithms, this requires "3f+1" replicas to be able to tolerate "f" failing nodes. As PBFT chooses a leader in round-robin fashion, nodes need to agree on a "membership list" of nodes to select from, originally picked by the company that designed the protocol (Curran 2018). When such an authority controls the list, the system is referred to by some as "centralized," no matter how many nodes are approved to operate. Essentially, every node is involved with every transaction to reach an agreed-on critical number, a quorum. Typically a BFT algorithm consists of a system with messages sent back and forth in a voting process, and consensus is achieved when over 66% of the nodes agree. Under proof of stake (PoS), the selected validators that are to suggest the next block for approval are chosen at random followed by multiround voting mechanisms typically based on stake in the system, as with the number of coins held. PoS BFT systems are significantly faster than PoW. Ripple pioneered a decentralized alternative algorithm called Federated Byzantine Agreement (FBA), and Stellar refined it to provide the first provably safe FBA protocol. Each entity decides on others it trusts, a so-called quorum slice. When these slices overlap sufficiently, it is a quorum, necessary to approve transactions. Unlike the earlier Byzantine Agreements, Stellar's FBA is free entry or open membership into validation. Ripple is semi-permissioned and stands between Stellar and the entirely permissioned blockchains of R3 Corda, Hyperledger, Ethereum, and Swift's version of distributed ledgers.

Here are the featured properties that distinguish these various systems. Again, fault tolerance means a protocol can survive failure of a validator at any point. Safety is a guarantee that something bad will never happen (e.g., no forks or partitions as multiple competing versions of truth), but under safety, if no consensus is reached, an auxiliary process is required to reboot. Liveness (as in availability) means the system is always in operation, even if there are faults or forks, making progress toward some eventual conclusion. PoW favors liveness over safety (forks are possible). The FBA system favors safety, as an accidental fork halts operations until fixed. Other distinctions have to do with latency and transaction speed. Bitcoin with PoW is slow and requires approximately six blocks of transactions groups on ledgers to be confirmed, asymptotically, which takes approximately an hour. For BFT and FBA protocols, with their message passing and voting, transactions are approved every three to five seconds. Asymptotic security means no amount of computing power can overcome consensus. Bitcoin does not have this. BFT and FBA are approved with private keys and ledgers-transaction-asymptotic security is achieved. Finally, validation systems may still be subject to collusion from bad actors. In Bitcoin, there is concern now with potential collusion among miners (as discussed below). In BFT protocols, over 66% of validators have to collude. In an FBA protocol, a complicated web of approval is thought to make collusion virtually impossible.

Among blockchain platforms that allow smart contracts, relevant here in the current discussion of alternative validation systems (and discussed again in chapter 6), are Hyperledger Fabric, Ethereum, Quorum, and Corda.

Hyperledger is modified according to the needs of enterprise. There is no one-size-fits-all. Hyperledger allows multiple consensus algorithms. Quorum, based on Ethereum, uses a peer-to-peer encrypted message exchange for transferring private data to network participants and offers consensus mechanisms that are appropriate for semiprivate consortium chains with controlled user groups. Finally, Corda is a permissioned ledgers system in which contacting parties name one or several nodes that are responsible for consensus (Sharma 2019).

## 5.5 Featured Examples

### 5.5.1 Bitcoin

Transactions in Bitcoin are encoded messages. The public and private keys ensure that no one can transact on someone else's ID, impersonating a node. Because the message or transaction can only be created with the key combination, it is known that the spender wishes to unlock and spend the coin. Plus, this brings commitment to the transaction, so it cannot be undone or reneged on later.

Double-spending would be possible if two messages from a given node were able to spend the same coin. In fact, with internet latency, the problem mentioned earlier, it would be hard to know who the victim is—that is, which transaction came first and should be valid in principle, as time stamps are not necessarily chronological. For Bitcoin, blocks of individual transactions are broadcast to the entire network, or at least to those listening among the community of users. Blocks economize on messages and costs of validation. Anonymous nodes verify blocks of new transactions of which they are aware, transactions that have been accumulating as candidates on individual copies of ledgers over the previous 10 minutes or so. The messages broadcast to the community of users consist of these new series of transactions on the block, concatenated with a randomly chosen number and then hashed into a 256-bit encrypted message. Hashing as noted earlier is a one-way function. To dis-encrypt the hash back into the message, one needs to proceed by trial and error, though solutions are evident once found. In this sense it is a random miner of the code who succeeds in inverting. In fact, a group of miners are all simultaneously running code to decipher and the miner that finds the solution first finds it essentially randomly, as everyone is attempting to find by trial and error. All of the blocks of ledgers in a chain are linked together, given that the top of each ledger contains the hash of the previous ledger. Cryptography with proof of work by these miners, implemented up to six times, ideally sends the probability of malfunction or fraud asymptotically to zero.

One potential problem is that nodes as bad actors could violate the protocol and propose the latest version of the ledger that they would like to become immutable (e.g., knowingly containing the second of the double-spend transactions while the first was already used to acquire something else). To thwart this, under the Bitcoin system, it is again as if one node were selected at random to certify a current new candidate ledger. There are thus two keys to Bitcoin. One is this certification, which requires time and energy. A proof-of-work algorithm requires a selectable amount of work to find the random number that, when added to the set of transactions, creates the hash. Difficulty is controlled. The discovered random number is then added to the bottom of the block as the proof of puzzle solved, a certification of work done that all can confirm easily. The work, which is costly in its use of electricity and equipment, limits entry into validation. The second key to Bitcoin, and a premise of computer science more generally, is that most nodes are honest, so the de facto randomly selected miner is likely to be honest and following the protocol.

Temporary multiplicity or fraud is possible if another branch containing new blocks is created. But the conventional protocol is that the longest interim chain is considered to be the valid one. To reinforce this, and not incidentally, here Satoshi Nakamoto (2008) put some economics into the design of the computer science protocol. Miners have incentives to mine the longest chain, as they are rewarded in Bitcoin only if the block of transactions they validate becomes, eventually, part of the immutable history. To repeat in crude terms: Validators now have pecuniary interests in the outcomes they are validating. (We shall come back in this idea in chapter 6.)

Some recent economics literature has provided critiques of Bitcoin.[4] Others argue the cryptocurrency protocol is more robust and malleable than it might seem. First, there could be threats of a double-spending run or extortion if a group of miners acquired 51% of computing power. The industry of miners is in fact quite concentrated, so this has been a concern.

Relatedly, Budish (2018) has argued that the expense of acquiring majority hash power is not an effective deterrent against double-spend attacks. To paraphrase Budish, the amount of computational power devoted to mining must satisfy (1) a zero-profit condition among miners, who engage in competition for the prize associated with adding the next block to the chain, and (2) a limited commitment or rationality constraint that the "stock" computational costs of such an attack must exceed the recurring "flow" payments to miners for running the blockchain, so that they stay in. The second constraint is less binding if (i) the mining technology used to run the blockchain is both scarce and non-repurposable and (ii) any majority attack is a "sabotage" in that it causes a collapse in the economic value of the blockchain. The latter is something close to Nakamoto's original argument.

Biais et al. (2018) model the proof-of-work blockchain protocol as a stochastic game and analyze the equilibrium strategies of rational, strategic miners. Mining the longest chain is a Markov perfect equilibrium, without forking, in line with Nakamoto (2008). But the blockchain protocol is a coordination game, with multiple equilibria. There exist equilibria with forks, leading to orphaned blocks and persistent divergence between chains.

Aronoff (2019) argues that a reorganization of the chain creating a fork will take at most a few hours to carry out and that the rental cost will be modest. Thus, what seems crucial for Budish's argument is that the flow of mining rewards will still lie above the rental value of investment in hash power. A further critique beyond this bound is that Budish's logic assumes there are no other responses.

> In fact the victim has the option to either accept the reversion to the chain or to carry out its own reorganization and negate the double-spend attack. Likewise, the attacker can either accept the failure of its attempted double-spend or respond by implementing a reorganization to re-instate the double-spend, and so on. (Aronoff 2019, 2)

### 5.5.2 Ripple

Closely related to the Kenyan environment where we featured transfers of value from city to town are cryptographic e-money systems for the purchase and sale of national currencies, including transfers of value across international borders. It is at present relatively costly and slow to do this transaction through commercial banking systems. Ripple is a for-profit entity that has revolutionized this environment by working with mainstream large financial institutions.

Users of Ripple buy the coin "XRP" and can make payments among each other using cryptographically signed transactions denominated in XRP. But transactions in fiat currencies and other objects without XRP are frequent. Fiat tokens represent fiat monies on the ledgers. Ripple is essentially a payments protocol for fiat money transfers through fiat tokens. XRP has value, but the company reasons that XRP is part of a design to prevent hacking. Flooding servers with innumerable transactions causes the XRP cost of transactions to rise exponentially, hence it is not a cost-effective strategy. Put differently, simply being malicious can be exorbitantly costly.

For XRP-denominated transactions, Ripple can make use of its internal ledger, and XRP can be sent to anyone. But a primary function is an interbank transfer system. Typically, financial institutions are key gateways trusted by users that hold funds and issue balances on behalf of customers. In that sense there has been limited entry into the Ripple system. A bank is able to lock fiat currency and transact with the associated fiat token on the Ripple network. Specifically, an issuance is a method for an individual account holder on the blockchain to "lock" a particular asset on the blockchain ledger. After an issuance is made it can be sent to other accounts, taking advantage of Ripple's low fees (Schuster 2017).

Trust lines are Ripple's way of securing transactions between individual parties after issuance. Users have to specify the other users they trust and to what amount. Furthermore, when a payment is made between two users that trust each other, the balance of the mutual credit line is adjusted, subject to limits set by each user. The user paying out to a customer in the country of destination is effectively lending value to the originator of the transaction, trusting to get this value back. This is similar to the medieval *hawala* system among merchants and correspondent banks, a popular and informal value-transfer system based not on the movement of cash or on telegraph or computer network wire transfers between banks, but instead on the performance and honor of a huge network of money brokers (known as *hawaladars*) (Wikipedia 2018a).

In order to send assets between users that have not directly established a trust relationship, the protocol tries to find a path between the two users such that each link of the path is between two users who do have a trust relationship, again subject to caps.[5] In principle, if there is not a trust path, then one can use XRP to balance the transaction in the other direction. Likewise, credit lines readjust to earlier levels if there are flows among trusted users going the other way. Outstanding IOUs are on a public ledger of accounts.

All transactions on the Ripple network need to be validated in the sense of agreeing to correctness and timing in order to prevent double-spending. Each Ripple server connects to a network of peers, relays cryptographically signed transactions, and maintains a local copy of the complete shared global ledger. A Ripple server running in validator mode additionally participates in the consensus process and is a part of an interconnected web of validators, each of whom trusts a specific set of validators not to collude.

A FBA algorithm relies on four rounds of sequential voting, starting at a 50% quorum and reaching 80%. This is termed the Ripple Protocol Consensus Algorithm. It seems from available descriptions that server nodes may have a stake in the transactions they are validating (XRP Ledger 2019).

### 5.5.3 Stellar, Featuring Entry

The Stellar Development Foundation is a not-for-profit organization that provides greater access and inclusion by connecting people to low-cost financial services. Stellar is open source and a public ledger: It sees expansion into underserved populations as its primary mission. Stellar does not rely on mainstream financial institutions. Individual users are not necessarily large financial institutions such as banks—that is, they are allowed to be nonbanks and small, such as money-transfer operators.

Stellar Consensus Protocol (SCP) (Mazieres 2016) uses a Federated Byzantine Agreement that allows more universal access, akin to the internet, as a way to interact among strangers. In the Stellar protocol for validation, each participant names others it considers important and requires that the majority of these others agree to any batch of transactions. Yet those other important participants do not agree until the participants they consider important also agree. Each transaction requires a majority of nodes designated as "important" by both traders (Ray 2018). The system is thus designed to be open to new entrants who name their own trust network. Unlike Bitcoin, Stellar forms a decentralized consensus among a group of nodes that are transitively connected to each other by trust.

Stellar, like Ripple, can transfer value across virtually any object (e.g., creating fiat money tokens that are then cashed out). Stellar can also transfer the tokens of others who wish to design their own platform with their own coin, linking to Stellar for value transfers.

Stellar uses anchors and market makers to intermediate the exchange of individual parties. An anchor is typically a highly regarded financial institution—namely, a commercial bank. This part is similar to Ripple. To make an international exchange transaction, for example, a customer makes a deposit with the anchor in the fiat currency of the country of origination, for example, and thus issues an IOU, a debt, to the depositor. This is termed a *base account*. The fiat money is then converted 1–1 to a token-equivalent amount, apart from fees, and these tokens are termed *assets* in a base account. The anchor contacts a market maker—a user who, like broker-dealers in other contexts, posts bid-ask spreads and carries some inventory of a variety of assets. If not holding the fiat token of the country of destination, a second broker-dealer acts as a go-between. An algorithm searches for minimal paths. Potentially finding the optimal path is an NP-hard problem, but typically only two steps are used, at most. The user broker-dealer needs to establish a trust line with the anchor to assure itself the deposit with the originating fiat money is there and that the asset is backed in that sense.

### 5.5.4 Recent Entrants

HotStuff is a practical Byzantine fault-tolerant protocol that replaces a mesh communication network with a star communication network (see figure 5.4). It will be used by Libra. This means each communication will rely on the leader. The node no longer broadcasts the message to other nodes but sends the

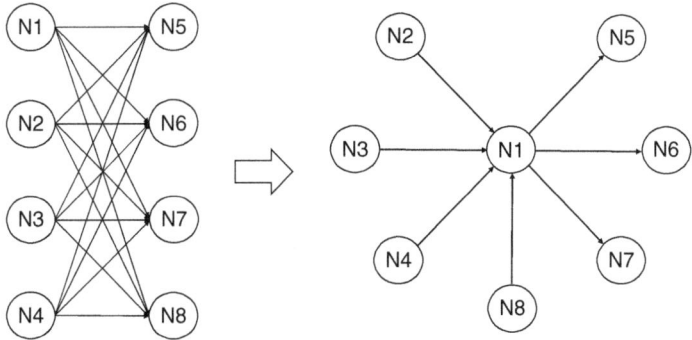

**Figure 5.4**
Mesh communication networks and star communication networks. The figure on the left shows how nodes *N* are connected to each other. The figure on the right displays a classic star network with a central node.
*Source:* Author.

message to the leader, which processes it and sends it to other nodes. Thus the communication complexity of the system is greatly reduced. Similar to PBFT, the leader proposes a state transition request and other nodes check its legitimacy after receiving the request.

Algorand uses a simple Byzantine agreement protocol with a leader. It is robust to latency and does not rely on the participants having synchronized clocks. Notably, Algorand takes into account the possibility of malicious leaders:

> When honest messages are delivered within a bounded worst-case delay, agreement is reached in an expected constant number of steps when the elected leader is malicious, and is reached after two steps when the elected leader is honest. (Chen et al. 2018, 1)

# 6
# Smart Contracts: Contract Theory and Mechanism Design

The relevance of contracts comes to life and is supercharged with the possibilities created by distributed ledger technology, which allows "smart contracts." Likewise, we can be more precise in this section about underlying frictions and how smart contracts can deal with them. Finally, we return to the diverse perspectives of mechanism design and computer science and find some unexploited common ground that could be used in subsequent designs.

## 6.1 Smart Contracts

At their most basic level, cryptocurrencies such as Bitcoin use a language familiar to accountants, economists, and computer scientists. The state of the system is the current ownership of a digital asset, the *stock*, and a transaction or transition is the change in its ownership, the *flow*. These stocks and flows are on ledgers. Bitcoin and the other validation systems are all about verifying and validating flows back to the genesis state where assets were originally created. This ties flows to stocks and requires verification of information.

Usually, though, the concept of ledgers is generalized to mean simply lists of "facts." Below we will draw on the language of the smart contract composer Corda. Everyone has a ledger, but it is synchronized and held in common only for shared facts. Consensus is broken into two pieces. Validity consensus means that a transition or transaction is accepted—that is, it has the required signatures, both for the current proposed transaction and for every transaction that led up to the proposed transaction. This is similar to the crypto-asset example. Unique consensus, in the language of Corda, is different and is the key to the generalization: A given party may not have a record of every single transaction, and that is not always required. There is not a consensus. On the other hand, a party could potentially request missing transaction information from notaries. The latter is necessary to thwart the double-spending problem, for example. The point here is that what is needed depends on the underlying environment and what the ledger is trying to accomplish, ideally as part of a constrained-optimal arrangement. Some transactions within a contract are private to the parties and there can be partitioning. Other transactions for value transfer may require public validation (more on the Corda notaries momentarily).

We have adopted in this section the language of Corda because it is perhaps the closest to the language of mechanism design, thus bringing computer science and economics together. That said, Ethereum is a well-known smart-contract protocol, close in its conception to Bitcoin, in which virtually all validations, even within a contract, are done by proof of work.

A contract is entered into by multiple parties. Parties are nodes. Identities of nodes could be anonymous, as in Bitcoin, but this is not required. Identities could be named and public—for example, the legal identity of an organization or the service identity of a network service. Note that trusted parties such as banks are allowed to be there as nodes, and to be public, but so too are others, as well as strangers. A node writing contracts is an app providing a service, which is also allowed to be a universal service, if desired. Technically, the smart contract itself is a node, but it is acting autonomously as per its code (as is made clear in the subsequent paragraph). The permissioned set of nodes for a given contract in Corda still has its access controlled by a doorman, so in that sense all contracts are only semiprivate, and there is a sense of "centralization."

The contract is a code that is validated initially. It either works or not, and one can imagine several independent validators of code, dealing with potentially malfunctioning nodes, which also link back to the Byzantine Generals Problem (bad actors) and to thwarting potential collusion. Ethereum validates all lines of code by proof-of-work consensus, but that is not required in other smart-contract composers (we will return to this subject later).

A contract agreement is made via public and private keys. After these initial validation steps, it becomes immutable. In this sense there is no reneging on whether agreements have been entered into, nor claims that they are written in a different way. There is no need for trust on these particular dimensions. It is clear to outsiders what the parties intended. Smart contracts are stored and executed on a distributed ledger, an electronic record that is updated in real time and intended to be maintained on geographically dispersed servers or nodes. Through decentralization, evidence of the smart contract and its execution can be deployed to some or all nodes on a network, which effectively prevents modifications not authorized or agreed to by the parties.

A contract specifies states at a point in time (current ownership, for example) or other facts. Communication under a contract is node to node, not necessarily broadcast to the entire public, as in Bitcoin, but on a need-to-know basis, as prespecified in the contract. An *oracle*, a term computer scientists use to denote a function or node that knows the answer, is used to verify known facts that are states of a contract. Commands initiate transfers and result in output states.

Corda allows a notary service for validation of communication and proposed transactions within the contract. Upon receiving a proposed transaction, the notary will either accept it, if the notary has not already signed other conflicting transactions, or will reject it, as would happen in an attempt to double-spend. Every state has an appointed notary, and a notary will only notarize a transaction if it is the appointed notary of all the transaction's input states. A notary may be a single network node, in which case this part is quite centralized and has a trusted-third-party aspect. Alternatively, there can be a cluster of mutually trusting nodes to deal with faults or mutually distrusting nodes to deal with incentives. Though some Corda applications have multiple notaries, this is more for latency issues, and the incentive motivation for multiple notaries is not evident. We come back to a merger of the computer science and economic points of view at the end of this chapter. Notaries can choose a consensus algorithm based on privacy, scalability, legal system compatibility, and algorithmic agility. A notary could decide not to provide validity consensus, though in some contexts this runs the risk of denial of state attacks.

The key capabilities of smart contracts are that they overcome underlying frictions. Smart contracts allow full commitment, immutability, conditionality, observability, and enforceability. We come back to these ideas in the subsequent sections.

Nick Szabo, the inventor of smart contracts, states the advantage succinctly: Smart contracts would enable both parties to observe the other's performance of the contract, guarantee that only the details necessary for completion of the contract are revealed to both parties, and be self-enforcing to eliminate the time spent policing the contract (Gord 2016).

Agents in a contract use digital signatures: Private cryptographic keys are held by each party to verify participation and assent to agreed-on terms. A smart contract will take actions (e.g., disperse payments), without further action by the counterparties, and they can access or refer to outside information or data to trigger actions.

Smart contracts fit naturally with elements of mechanism design; that is, they allow the execution of the kinds of contracts and mechanisms that economists have largely taken for granted: the revelation principle, enduring relationships, promised utilities, resolutions of the hold-up problem, and trusted reputation. We now elaborate on each of these in turn.

## 6.2 Mechanism Design

### 6.2.1 Messages

A game or mechanism among players is a specification of messages that can be sent, message spaces, and an allocation rule mapping realized messages onto outcomes such as transfers. Consider a Bayesian Nash equilibrium of such a mechanism, with strategies for play in which the strategy of any party to the contract is to maximize taking—that is, given the maximizing strategies of others, taking expectations relative to given information. The *revelation principle* asserts that for any given game with abstract message spaces and allocation rules, there is an alternative game in which messages can be reduced to statements about underlying unobserved facts and private information, and in this new, modified game, agents have incentives to tell the truth about privately observed states. This is without loss of generality (Harris and Townsend 1981; see also Dasgupta, Hammond, and Maskin 1979 and Myerson 1982). There are three interrelated points. The first point is that messages would be transmitted by actors or nodes and put on distributed ledgers. A second, related point is that the messages become endogenous objects. We have moved from how to design database and communication systems to the incentives that create the underlying data to be transmitted. Third, messages are truthful, because of underlying incentives, and so

**Box 6.1**
Key elements from mechanism design.

### Single period contract with messages

There are two agents: #1 a villa as an agent, who observes a vector $\theta$ of its current state (e.g., its harvest output), and #2, the central estate as principal, who does not see it. Under this resource allocation scheme, villa 1 waits to see output vector $\theta$ before sending message $m$. Thus its decision problem is of the form, for every $\theta \in \theta$, maximize $U^1[\theta - f(m)]$ by choice of $m \in M$. The agent sends a message $m$ about the value of $\theta$ to the principal, choosing $m$ from a set of possible messages $M$ agreed to in the contract, and as a function of the message sent, is taxed, or receives a transfer if negative, $f(m)$, to the principal.

### Multi-period contracts: histories and immutability

A two-period contract (with randomized rewards) occurs when agent 1 at date $t=2$, given some history of announcements at $t=1$, $\tilde{\theta}_1$, is given incentives to announce current actual $\theta_2$ truthfully as opposed to any counterfactual value $\tilde{\theta}_2$. These messages result in lottery $\pi(\tau)$ over transfers $\tau$, and expected utility is the metric payoff for agent 1:

$$\Sigma_\tau U^1[\theta_2 - \tau]\pi_2\left(\tau \mid \tilde{\theta}_1, \theta_2\right) \geq \Sigma_\tau U^1[\theta_2 - \tau]\pi_2\left(\tau \mid \tilde{\theta}_1, \tilde{\theta}_2\right). \quad (1)$$

The history of announcements $\tilde{\theta}_1$ is public and immutable. Working the dynamic program backward to $t=1$, agent 1 is given incentives to announce actual $\theta_1$ truthfully, as distinct from some other $\tilde{\theta}_1$, taking into account that agent 1 will want to be truthful at date 2, as derived in equation (1).

The incentive constraints at date 1, for every actual $\theta_1$ and announced $\tilde{\theta}_1$, are presented as

$$\begin{aligned}&\Sigma_\tau U^1[\theta_1 - \tau]\pi_1(\tau \mid \theta_1) + \beta\Sigma_{\theta_2} p(\theta_2 \mid \theta_1)\Sigma_\tau U^1[\theta_2 - \tau]\pi_2(\tau \mid \theta_1, \theta_2) \\ &\geq \Sigma_\tau U^1[\theta_1 - \tau]\pi_1(\tau \mid \tilde{\theta}_1) + \beta\Sigma_{\theta_2} p(\theta_2 \mid \theta_1)\Sigma_\tau U^1[\theta_2 - \tau]\pi_2(\tau \mid \tilde{\theta}_1, \theta_2).\end{aligned} \quad (2)$$

In equation (2), $p(\theta_2 \mid \theta_1)$ is the probability of $\theta_2$ conditioned on $\theta_1$.

do not need to be validated other than for the reliability of the computers that send the messages. This separates the external validation problem from the internal contract part, a hugely beneficial step.

As an example, consider an economy with one period, two agents, and multiple commodities or multiple financial assets. One agent's shocks to utility or its value function for profits determine the trade-off in the objects it wants to consume or assets held, but these shocks are not seen by the other party. The other party is, however, in this example, indifferent to the various combinations of what is consumed or held. The first agent with private information sends messages announcing the agent's preference shocks to the second party, messages that are part of the ledger. The outcome function specifies transfers of goods, hence requiring shipment, and/or transfers of securities, which can be done online in registries. The first agent has an internal incentive to send the correct, truthful message, because the agent bears all the consequences of its announcement.

### 6.2.2 Impact of Enduring Relationships (Duration): Past History of Messages Becomes Committed and Creates a New State as Part of the Determination of Contemporary Outcomes

Distributed ledgers housing smart contracts can help to implement formal and enduring relationships (Townsend 1982) that extend over time. The idea as indicated earlier is to give a household, firm, or trader an incentive to reveal private information. Sometimes we take this for granted. A household with low but privately observed income will have an incentive to implicitly announce or reveal low income by the act of requesting a loan, assuming here for the moment that loans must be paid back in the next period and that this is not an issue. Conditionality with collateral can ensure repayment, but there are other means to ensure repayment, which we address below. To return to the main thread, the opposite outcome holds for households with high income today that voluntarily invest, with more funds coming back, available for the next period.

A bit more formally, we can imagine an economy with two agents, one borrowing/investing with variable income and a second who is willing to enter into the contract. The first agent has variable endowments over time and is risk averse, caring about ex ante expected utility. The second is risk neutral with essentially unlimited deterministic resources. Income realizations of the first agent are not public. The two agents agree and enter into a contract at some initial date, and it is then carried out over time. Though borrowing and lending form an incentive-compatible contract with private information, it is not the best that can be done. The optimal information-constrained arrangement is a blend of borrowing/lending and insurance. The constrained-optimal contract contains more risk contingencies in the contract relative to borrowing and lending, as the contract is entered into before the underlying state is known, allowing some insurance against the state. If income is low, for example, the borrowing agent acquires more money than from borrowing alone, as if an indemnity for low income is paid, and this agent faces a lower inter-temporal interest rate on the loan to be repaid. In turn, if income is high, the agent pays in an ex post premium, receiving some lesser amount of money back the next period. Longer contracts are better.[1]

A two-period or longer-term relationship contract is implemented using messages of unobserved states that are validated and put on a consensus ledger. For example, past messages of high- or low-income states both determine the outcome in the current period, pay out or receive, but also the state for the next period. That is, future pay receive, pay-in schedules are conditioned on current messages as well as messages in the next period.

### 6.2.3 Promised Utility as the State

To generalize, and thinking of longer-term relationships, the contract payoff can be divided into two pieces. One piece is a contemporary reward or penalty today, with goods, money, and/or tokens changing hands as a function of the message today. The other piece is the discounted expected utility of continued participation from the next period onward, varying with the outcome and action.[2] This expected utility is the key state variable to be entered on ledgers as a state variable for tomorrow triggered by states as messages today. Beginning-of-period promised utility is the state of the contract. The messages satisfy truth-telling or incentive constraints, so there is no need for trust other than presumed maximization. These utility numbers are under full control of the long-term contract, and here in this example they are public, with the conditional possibilities for future periods a function of such facts/states. The idea is to create incentives to announce states truthfully.

### 6.2.4 Incentives to Take Appropriate Action

An example that is explicit about unobserved actions taken in a contract is a multi-period, principal-agent insurance problem. The agent is a household or firm that enters into a contract with a risk-neutral insurer. The agent can take an action that makes loss less likely or profits higher, but this action is not seen by the insurer. If full insurance against loss or profit fluctuation were agreed to, the agent would have no incentive to take a costly action, hence the term *moral hazard*. This is indeed the classic moral-hazard problem (Harris and Raviv 1979). The constrained-optimal contract does not provide full insurance or zero insurance. Instead, it balances off the gains from insurance against this distortion in actions. If final losses or profits are fully observed, though again the action is not, the optimal contract culminates with a state-contingent transfer from the

**Box 6.2**
Dynamic principal and agent problem with moral hazard and promised utility.

> The dynamic optimal contracting problem between a risk-neutral lender and the household is described as follows. The value function $V(w, k)$ of the principal is the discounted expected present value of the dynamic contract from the current state, promised utility $w$ to the agent and capital $k$ of agent, choosing a mixture or lottery over current transfer $\tau$ to the agent, induced effort $z$ on the part of the agent, observed output $q$ from the firm run by the agent, an assignment of promised utility for the next period $w'$, and investment, hence next period capital stock $k'$. The $V(w, k)$ is the contemporary award to the principal, $q - \tau$, and pay off next period $V(w', k')$ discounted by the outside economy-wide gross interest rate $R$.
>
> $$V(w, k) = \max_{\{\pi(\tau, q, \bar{z}, k', w'|k, w)\}} \sum_{T \times Q \times Z \times K' \times W'} \pi(\tau, q, z, k', w'|k, w)$$
> $$[q - \tau + \left(\frac{1}{R}\right) V(w', k')]$$
>
> Consistency in promises requires as a constraint that previous promises resulting in current state $w$ must be consistent with the utility earned by the agent with contemporary utility function $U$, receiving transfers while in control of the capital stock, partially depleted by deprecation rate $\delta$ and adjusted for capital carried over to the next period. Effort $z$ enters into contemporary utility as a negative disutility term. The agent discounts the future at rate $\beta$, pre-multiplying next period promised utility $w'$, a control variable of the contract.
>
> **Promise-keeping**
>
> $$\sum_{T \times Q \times Z \times K' \times W'} \pi(\tau, q, z, k', w'|k, w) [U(\tau + (1 - \delta)k - k', z) + \beta w'] = w.$$
>
> There are additional Bayes rule consistency, adding-up, and nonnegativity constraints.
>
> Incentive compatibility is ensured by the moral-hazard constraint that the agent should take the action $\bar{z}$ recommended under the contract,

with utility on the left-hand side of the inequality, as distinct from any other action $\hat{z}$ resulting in utility on the right-hand side of the inequality, where if $\hat{z}$ were taken, the probability of output $q$ given $k$ has to be adjusted according to a likelihood ratio.

**Moral hazard**

Additional constraints are incentive compatible, $\forall (\bar{z}, \hat{z}) \in Z \times Z$.

$$\sum_{T \times Q \times K' \times W'} \pi(\tau, q, \bar{z}, k', w' | k, w) \left[ U(\tau + (1-\delta)k - k', \bar{z}) + \beta w' \right]$$
$$\geq \sum_{T \times Q \times K' \times W'} \pi(\tau, q, \bar{z}, k', w' | k, w) \frac{P(q|\hat{z}, k)}{P(q|\bar{z}, k)} \left[ U(\tau + (1-\delta)k - k', \hat{z}) + \beta w' \right]$$

insurer to the agent as a function of those observables. If losses or profits are unobserved, the agent must be given an incentive to tell the truth in messages as well, as discussed earlier. If the relationship does not terminate, then in addition to the current transfer, promised utility is updated for the next period. Essentially the agent takes into account rewards in terms of both higher current consumption (dividends) and higher future utility, and vice versa, with penalties for low states.

### 6.2.5 Utility Threats

Fernandes and Phelan (2000) generalize with unobserved past states to include yet another dimension: utility threats. There are upper bounds for what one can get if one has deviated in the past and contemplates lying or disobedience now. The threat bounds are high enough to keep agents on the equilibrium path so that there is no deviation in the first place.

If we are capturing the underlying economic environment accurately, these expected utility numbers or utility threats will indeed be the actual realized subjective utility an agent would experience, or get in the event of deviation, in that environment under the incentive scheme. This is also a qualification. If the approximation of the model to the actual economic environment is poor, then these promised utilities and threats in the contract will be poor approximations of actual subjective utility.

### 6.2.6 Costly State Verification: Limited Message Spaces and No Need for Validation

As a third example on this theme, output from a project is privately observed but verification of project output by a lender or insurer is possible at a cost. In effect, this is a costly verification of the underlying situation that generated the messages and hence in principle could be part of computer science designs. Over a range of outputs, repayment of a loan is constant, resembling debt. Actual outcomes need not be known, and in effect there is no message and no need for validation. For low outputs, however, claims are verified at a cost, as if validating financial statements, for example. This is costly state verification (Townsend 1979; Gale and Hellwig 1985).

### 6.2.7 Various Meanings of the Word "Trust" in Economics, as Distinct from Limited Commitment

The general point here is that the word "trust" in mechanism design has various meanings—trust that an agent will announce unobserved states—but more likely this agent is given an incentive to do so, as a result of intra-temporal or inter-temporal considerations. Similarly, there could be trust that an agent will take appropriate actions, but more likely the agent is given an incentive to do so by reward schedules. In particular, incentives are separated from full commitment, the promise to do something regardless, as distinct concepts. Full commitment without incentives is akin to naïve communication protocols followed by trusted agents. To be fair, all the above examples are presumed to have some full commitment on the part of the parties to carry out the agreement—that is, pay for goods transfers or repay a loan, without reneging.

To elaborate, the simplest of contracts between two parties is the purchase and sale of a commodity or asset. Indeed, if done as a spot-market exchange, then we can avoid the language of contracts altogether. But here it is clarifying to think of the contract as an agreement on the part of the buyer to surrender cash and the seller to surrender the commodity. More generally, the buyer is debited cash and the seller is credited. When there are lags between the time of the agreement to trade and the eventual payment, then issues can arise. If there were no collateral, then the parties have to trust each other to carry out their part, pay cash or ship goods. This is a full-commitment contract under which promises are made and honored, as is commonly assumed in the contract literature, hence, one notion of trust. However, an alternative is for a trusted third party to stand between the traders making trade possible among strangers. PayPal and Alibaba/Ant Financial are examples.

With borrowing and lending, trust issues are even more apparent, as the lender either trusts the borrower to repay or, otherwise, the collateral backing the loan should be placed in escrow. In the latter case, a transaction among strangers is possible, implemented with a conditional if-then statement to define what happens with and without default; see Geanakoplos (2003) and Kilenthong and Townsend (2018) for a literature on securities as contracts that embed collateral as a contract characteristic.

In contrast, under limited commitment without a third-party intermediary and without collateral, one party may wish to withdraw and go their own way as the contract unfolds. In this case contracts with limited commitment make sure that future rewards do not fall below certain thresholds, in order to retain participation. This is loaded into the underlying contract itself. In the autarky version of this, there is implicit trust that a banishment penalty can be imposed were withdrawal to happen. Ironically, it takes this off-equilibrium commitment to deal with the original limited-commitment problem.[3]

For example, in a multiparty insurance arrangement, an agent with realized high income is supposed to pay an ex post premium, as a gift to others, into the insurance pool. But continued participation may yield lower interim expected utility for that agent than not paying and going it alone. These

**Box 6.3**
Limited commitment.

---

An additional constraint is appended to the equations for box 6.2. Let $v^{\text{aut}}(k')$ be the discounted utility from the next period on if the agent takes capital $k'$ into autarky on their own. Let $\Omega(k, q, z)$ be the utility at the point of withdrawal, with current capital $k$ given, effort $z$ taken, and $q$ realized, plus discounted $v^{\text{aut}}(k')$. The limited-commitment constraint ensures that with $\bar{q}$ and $\bar{z}$ given, if the agent stays in, expected utility as determined by transfers and promises for tomorrow and next period's capital is not less than the utility of withdrawal into autarky, defined above.

Additional constraints, limited commitment, for all $(\bar{q}, \bar{z}) \in Q \times Z$, are

$$\sum_{T \times K' \times W'} \pi(\tau, \bar{q}, \bar{z}, k', w' | k, w) [u(\tau + (1-\delta)k - k', \bar{z}) + \beta w'] \geq \Omega(k, \bar{q}, \bar{z}),$$

where $\Omega(k, q, z)$ is the present value of the agent going to autarky with the agent's current output at hand $q$ and capital $k$, which is defined as

$$\Omega(k, \bar{q}, z) \equiv \max_{k' \in K'} \{u(\bar{q} + (1-\delta)k - k', \bar{z}) + \beta v^{\text{aut}}(k')\},$$

where $v^{\text{aut}}(k)$ is the autarky-forever value.

participation constraints, as limited-commitment constraints, are now part of the original contracting problem. In effect, when a bound is hit, the contract resets so that the party tempted to renege gets more out of the arrangement.

Likewise, in the competitive market version of this, we trust a party not to break the relationship even though it might be advantageous not only to one of the original parties to the contract but also to an entrant. Specifically, one party of a contract is drawn off by a competitor or a third party that has not entered into the original, multi-agent arrangement (Jacklin 1987). Relatedly, even within the arrangement, both parties to a contract may wish to renegotiate and start over, but that would be bad for incentives ex ante. So, either the parties trust that will not happen, as in full-commitment models, or a time-consistency constraint is appended to the underlying contract problem so that there is no temptation.[4] Enhanced commitment to deal with single-party or multiple-party deviations is possible under the smart-contract technology.

### 6.2.8 Reputation

Otherwise, if contracts are incomplete and penalties cannot be imposed internally as part of the contract, then there is a way to formalize a role for reputation when there is no trust. There is a way to design and commit to optimal social penalties through a scoring function (Lehnert, Ligon, and Townsend 1999). This kind of indirect scoring does improve commitment in the broader sense. The notion that we trust third parties because we know they are worried about their reputations is formalized in this literature. It is not taken for granted. It is modeled and is part of the design. Nodes can be given incentives to validate correctly, for example. With these in place we have trust, but a more nuanced version—in effect something like trust but verify, as in nuclear disarmament. Here, it is trust but it is implemented through scoring. One can "trust" third parties without thinking all this through, but obviously things can go awry.

### 6.2.9 The Economics of Collusion and How to Prevent It

We have been discussing how to find constrained-efficient, ex ante agreements via maximization subject to truth-telling constraints, moral-hazard constraints, and limited-commitment constraints. However, though a solution exists and constitutes a valid (Bayesian) Nash equilibrium, typically the solution is not immune to collusion. That is, players need not act in the Nash sense of taking the strategies of others as given, but rather could all act in concert to enhance their welfare at the expense of the principal. One example is the discussion of Bitcoin miners discussed previously. Another example would be auctions where agents can collude in their bids. So either we trust parties not to collude or, as can now be anticipated, we place additional constraints on the multiparty contracts. The main point: These kinds of multiparty conditioning statements can be programmed under smart-contract technologies. The outcome is an explicit, contracted function of what each player says or does, in potentially complicated ways, so that deviations from a proposed collusion solution dominate (i.e., eliminate collusion).[5]

### 6.2.10 Implementation through Sequential Play: Loading in Commitment That Was Missing Previously

Holden and Malani (2018) examine how to use the blockchain mechanism to resolve the hold-up problem in economics: ex post bargaining when the contract is incomplete, without commitment. In their scheme, choices that cannot be verified by a third party can be resolved by a blockchain mechanism that can commit the parties to not engage in renegotiations. The keys here are the posting of agreements, having them notarized by multiple parties as witnesses, and the security and inalterability of the blockchain. Moore and Repullo (1988) and Maskin and

Tirole (1999) resolve an implementation problem using a simple sequential mechanism, as in Moore (1992): When one party tells the truth, that party earns more than if they lie. Joshua Gans (2018) shows how this implementation mechanism can be achieved with smart contracts to solve a trade problem.

### 6.2.11 Ledgers of the Financial Accounts

Contracts interface with ledgers and standard financial accounts. An asset as collateral in escrow is not really the same as an individually owned asset, as another party has a contingent claim on it. A special accounting is required. Likewise, it is natural to think of the flow of future wage payments as human capital on the balance sheet, which is a standard view in some sense (Aiyagari 1994; Huggett and Kaplan 2015). Smart contracts on the distributed ledger allow an immutable commitment that future income flows be sequestered as collateral. A modified accounting needs to be implemented. These two components of distributed ledgers—accounts and contracts—are interacting.

## 6.3 Smart Contracts in Computer Science and Incentives in Economics: Contrasts, Similarities, and Problems in Implementation

Though the language of smart contracts and the language of mechanism design fit remarkably well with each other, there are some key differences. Many of these differences came up in the previous section but bear repeating. In economics we try to avoid *a priori* classifications of trust. Individual agents are self-interested and optimize given their information and incentives, whereas nodes in computer science are trustworthy or not, or trusted up to a limit. Their role is often stated in simplistic terms—to validate whether or not a transaction is valid. Insofar as possible, we should be clear about this difference across the disciplines and take advantage of the strength of the two approaches. This means taking into account economic incentives in validation and potentially separating functionality into segregated components. There remain some key challenges in the interface.

To begin, there are other related differences: In economics it is a natural part of the design to give incentives to agents to be honest and obedient, as a function of the social context—that is, the purpose for which one is using the ledgers. In economics, writing out contracts as fully as possible is largely regarded as desirable, if it is possible.[6] In computer science, though, code is acknowledged to be "buggy," and hence it can be argued that simplicity has a special virtue. In economics, commitment is desirable if attainable, and renegotiation and bargaining are likely to change outcomes in an adverse way. In computer science, with its tendency to seek consensus and validate transactions in real time, the door is open to limited commitment, hence to more limited arrangements. This problem can be alleviated by separating internal contract and external validation incentives.

As in Narayanan and Weinberg (2018), there is a sparsity of hybrid models that occupy this middle ground between Nakamoto's dichotomy—that is, honest as opposed to malicious nodes, on one extreme, versus all players being potentially strategic, as in economics, at the other extreme. Narayanan and Weinberg think of cryptocurrencies as mechanisms and propose a protocol that must incentivize compliance for miners. They note that, for the most part, existing protocols are not incentive compatible. We provided some examples of this literature on the incentives for miners earlier.

### 6.3.1 Coding and Implementation Costs

On the downside, smart-contract coding can contain errors and has been difficult to use. Remedies are under development: Agrello is an initiative for human-readable smart contracts; iOlite has been developed to write smart contracts in natural language.

Smart contracts can be costly to implement, especially if initial validation of code, messages, and datasets are all put out for validation. In particular, calculations of gas charges to cover electricity costs in proof of work for Ethereum appear daunting.

Here is an example, from Nicolas Zhang (2019), focused on the coding cost. For context one can refer back to figure 2.1. There are two agents, A and B, with off-chain balance sheets that are not known to the other party. They face some balance-sheet shocks throughout time. If one agent is facing a positive shock, then there are excess reserves to invest. If one agent is facing a negative shock, then some liquidity is needed. The two agents wish to write a global smart contract that will function over time as situations evolve. They wish to implement the solution (a transfer function) on-chain.

The two agents first design a smart contract. Furthermore, imagine the two parties share their utility functions truthfully. This leaves an optimization problem to be solved, and the solver is the smart contract. Here, this seems a bit artificial. If the goal is borrowing/lending on the part of a first party with a second party only, then the desired amounts for borrowing or investing that the first party wants would be sufficient, as the other party always goes along (assuming no default). But in more complicated situations (e.g., a two-period, hybrid borrowing/lending insurance contract), the two agents would need to calculate what they want to do. That is carried into the example here, though, again, in a simplified context.

Suppose the solution to the borrowing/lending problem is not analytic (i.e., is not a closed-form solution and is solved by first-order-condition approximations). The derivatives are approximated by small, discrete differences depending on the size of a grid. The number of subtractions to form these differences is the dimensional of the discretized function domain (less one), and we are ignoring division.

In Ethereum there are costs to computing the derivative this way

(a) To form differences: gas × the dimensionality of the discretized function domain grid.

Next, try to set the derivative close to zero, hence

(b) To find local optima, a set of equality comparisons: 3 gas × the dimensionality of the discretized function domain grid.

Next

(c) To find the global optimum, a set of greater than equal comparisons: 2 gas × number of local optima.

Plus, in Ethereum, there is a one-time cost of implementing the smart contract. Add some cost during the life of the contract when it is called (for instance, updating every week, of every quarter, depending on the frequency the agents want).

In summary,

$G_{create}$ 3200 paid for a CREATE operation.
$G_{create}$ 200 paid per byte for a CREATE operation to succeed in placing code into state.
$G_{call}$ 700 paid for a CALL operation.

Given that the gas limit on Ethereum is 8,000,000 gas, even for something as easy as a borrowing and lending contract with a 1000-point discretized grid for the utility function domain, only 30 to 50 specifications of utility would fill an Ethereum block.

Thus, for more complicated optimization problems running only a few contracts (number of realized economic environments), blocks and costs would be higher. Of course, these costs come down significantly under alternative smart-contract protocols.

The next step is the sending of messages under the contract. Again figure 2.1 can be helpful. These messages can be verified on-chain as in the validation protocols, now an exact application. There is some cost, especially with proof of work. However, the messages themselves would be incentive compatible, by design of the optimization problem with appropriate constraints, so the validation has simply to do with whether messages are faulty or not received. We turn to this in the material below.

Finally, some transactions data (e.g., data of past messages) can be secured off-chain. After initial creation, the document is encrypted and validated on a blockchain so there is a time-stamped immutable record to prevent tampering. Any attempt to change the underlying database relative to the original would be apparent even if the change itself were not evident. One particular instance is the InterPlanetary File System (IPFS), a peer-to-peer distributed ledger system (IPFS 2019). A file, and all of the blocks within it, is given a unique fingerprint, which is its *cryptographic hash*. To look up a file to view or download, the network finds the nodes that are storing the content behind that file's hash. Each network node stores only content it is interested in, plus some indexing information that helps figure out which node is storing what.[7]

### 6.3.2 Reliability of Messages

Another potential problem has to do with the reliability of messages. A relevant insight: The revelation principle can be established in many contexts even though message transmission and receipt can both be noisy; despite the noise, one may as well let the computer transmit the message to the network the way it would have been sent originally, under the original game and message space.

Prescott (2003) extends the revelation principle to the situation of zero communication in a principal-agent context (i.e., no message is sent at all). This impacts the design of the incentive contract and is in some sense a worst-case scenario, but it does completely avoid the cost of validation.

Going in the other direction, the implementation problem of Harris and Townsend (1981) is a way of letting common private information be public by having multiple agents announce underlying states. Without noise in messages, at least, having two agents with common information announce that information is sufficient, in a well-designed payoff matrix, to make information public. Intuition would suggest that if messages are noisy, more agents announcing is better, but of increasingly limited value.

This brings us back to the notion of fault tolerance, which allows for a fraction of nodes to communicate inaccurately, as in distributed computing, either through machine error or, in the computer science literature what often seems to be taken as equivalent, because the node is deliberately malicious. Here we will discuss in more detail this distinction, which can be key.

The basic problem is a version of the Byzantine Generals Problem. Two generals must coordinate an attack for it to be successful. One sends a message to the other but cannot be sure the message has arrived. So the second general, knowing this, sends a confirmation, but in turn cannot be sure it has arrived. No finite number of iterations is ever sufficient for there to be complete certainty. In another version, the message may be received but inaccurately. In a third version, the message is accurate but the message could have been sent by a traitor, again mixing up computer inaccuracy with malicious behavior.

Rubinstein (1989) focuses on and formalizes a closely related electronic mail problem as a coordination problem. He draws a connection to the Byzantine Generals Problem in a concluding section. Two players have to play one of two possible coordination games. Only one player receives information about the coordination game to be played. If the players follow an obvious intuitive-communication protocol, then it is impossible for there ever to be common knowledge about the true state. Furthermore, the situation with "almost common knowledge" after a large number of successful messages remains different when compared with the coordination game played under common knowledge. This counterintuitive result shows that formalization with the logic of game theory can lead to surprises.

Morris and Shin (1997) build on this idea, drawing a key distinction between strategic and nonstrategic behaviors. Here is their version of the Byzantine Generals Problem, which is close to Halpern and Moses (1990):

> Two divisions of an army, each commanded by a general, are camped on two hilltops overlooking a valley. In the valley awaits the enemy. The commanding general of the first division has received a highly accurate intelligence report informing him of the state of readiness of the enemy. It is clear that if the enemy is unprepared and both divisions attack the enemy simultaneously at dawn, they will win the battle, while if either the enemy is prepared or only one division attacks, the attack will be defeated. If the first division general is informed that the enemy is unprepared, he will want to coordinate a simultaneous attack. But the generals can communicate only by means of messengers and, unfortunately, it is possible that a messenger will get lost or, worse yet, be captured by the enemy. (Morris and Shin 1997, 174)

Morris and Shin (1997) proceed in steps. They begin, as did Rubinstein (1989), with an imposed, simple, naïve communication protocol and a fixed objective. The fixed objective, the occasionally successful coordinated attack, though this may not be achieved, is defined as follows: (1) it is never the case that an attack occurs when the enemy is prepared; (2) it is never the case that one division attacks alone; and (3) both divisions sometimes successfully coordinate an attack.

The protocol allows back-and-forth communication: If the first division general hears that the enemy is unprepared, he sends a message to the second division general with the instruction "attack." If that first message arrives, the second division general sends a messenger with a confirmation that the first message was safely received. If the confirmation is delivered without mishap, the first division general sends another message to the second division general informing him of this fact.

To fill out the structure, suppose that with probability $\delta > 0$ the enemy is prepared, while with probability $1 - \delta$, the enemy is unprepared. The first division general knows which of these two contingencies is true, while the second division general does not. Each messenger gets lost with independent probability $\varepsilon < \delta$. Suppose that a successful attack has a payoff of 1 for the generals, while an attack that is unsuccessful is disastrous (either because the enemy is prepared or only one division attacks) and has a payoff of $-M$ for the generals, where $M$ is very large. An action protocol for the generals is optimal, given the communication protocol, if it maximizes the generals' expected payoff.

The first result: If the communication system is sufficiently reliable, then the optimized action protocol coordinates an attack almost always when the enemy is unprepared. Specifically, the first general attacks when the enemy is unprepared, even if he has not received a message confirmation from the second general. The second general attacks if he has received one message from the first general. Morris and Shin (1997) show this sequence dominates any other action protocols. For example, it dominates when the first general always attacks when the enemy is unprepared and the second always attacks, and also dominates when each general attacks if the second receives a message from the first and the first has received a confirmation of that message from the second.

But the above optimal action protocol turns out to be sensitive to a natural strategic concern, formalized as an equilibrium outcome in an incomplete-information game, with payoffs specified for each party as a function of that party's action and the action of the other general. In particular, off-diagonal elements give a payoff of $-M$ to the general that attacks alone regardless of whether the enemy is prepared. The previous protocol can be relied on if the generals choose to follow it. Is this what trusted nodes do? Nodes that are not (even) malicious? Not necessarily. Again from Morris and Shin (1997), suppose that the first division general knows that the enemy is unprepared, sends a message to the second division general, but receives no confirmation. He may be tempted to not commit his division to the battle in these circumstances as the probability is greater than one-half that his message was never received. In turn, given this and following the natural logic, the second division general may hesitate to attack if he has not received a reconfirmation from the first division general. In the strategic coordinated-attack problem with the naïve communication protocol, neither general ever attacks. Ironically, this happens if the communication system is sufficiently reliable.

What is the intuition? Each general must have an incentive to attack once he is actually called on to do so. Generals in the strategic game are not allowed to *commit* to strategies before the communication stage. Second, the generals have *different* objectives—the first division general would much rather that the second division attack alone than that the first division attack alone. Both these features are necessary for the paradox.

Relatedly, the communication protocols matter. Morris and Shin (1997) consider a revised "simple communication protocol" that builds in a kind of commitment. Suppose that if the enemy is unprepared, the first division general sends one message to the second division general informing him of this state of affairs. The second division general sends no confirmation (i.e., he is not allowed to communicate back). For sufficiently small $\varepsilon$, a coordinated attack almost always occurs whenever the enemy is unprepared.

This then raises the obvious larger issue: If one could design the communication system, subject to unavoidable communication errors that would be used by players in a strategic environment, how would it be done? Chwe's (1995) notion of "strategic reliability" is consistent with the discussion above: The design goal shifts from maximizing connectedness (or other measures of network reliability) to maximizing the likelihood that agents communicating over a flawed network can achieve desired outcomes via equilibria in the induced game. Multiple channels can facilitate collective action via redundancy, the sending of the same message along multiple paths or else repeatedly along the same path (Chwe 1995; De Jaegher and van Rooij 2011).

Coles and Shorrer (2012) examine how this logic extends to multiplayer settings where one informed agent serves as a "leader," relaying messages to and from the other parties. They show that the multiple channels may permit collective action: Parties may be able to coordinate their actions when messages arrive at their destinations in a sufficiently correlated fashion, as they would be if transmitted from a common sender. This also permits cutoff equilibria, where players take action after receiving a minimum number of confirmations.

In summary, though the consensus protocols outlined in chapter 5 deal with trust and seem to allow nontrusted or malicious parties, motivated by the Byzantine Generals Problem, they are not necessarily robust to natural strategic considerations. That is, they do not take the step of formalizing validation as strategic behavior in an incomplete-information game and may not be implementing an optimally designed communication system.

# 7

# Design Issues: Partitioned Ledgers, the Decision to Decentralize Implementation in Multiparty Contracts, and Incentive-Compatible Token Payment Systems

This chapter considers private information and partitioned ledgers, delegation of authority to a third-party platform, and tokens as communication devices.

## 7.1 Permissioned Private Ledgers and Gains from Concealment

In many environments, "unique consensus" is not desirable even if it were technologically possible. This is a generic implication of private information for optimal contract design. Though private information is effectively reported via messages or indirectly by choice and display options, this does not mean that such internal message data should be made public on the ledger. Often, the opposite is true: Messages should be kept private. Of course, cryptography with partitioned ledgers makes this possible.

Distributed ledger technology allows partitioning, but it does not have to be done in a mechanical way or, indeed, in the most extreme way often proposed—namely, by keeping all proprietary information entirely private. Likewise, an instance when all messages are made public means that the parties to the contract would see them, undercutting welfare. Neither of these extremes, all private versus all public, is typically constrained optimal.

Suppose shocks are to preferences and not to endowments. That is, agents are either urgent or patient to consume. This is the standard specification in modeling financial institutions or trade in financial markets. The Diamond and Dybvig (1983) model of banks and runs has versions of this exactly. The Duffie, Gârleanu, and Pedersen (2005) model of over-the-counter (OTC) trade in securities and consumption has stochastically varying security holding costs that motivate the trade. More generally, banks and traders face shocks to their portfolios that arise from the needs of their customers.

As an example, table 7.1 considers an economic environment with two parties to a contract with heterogeneous and random preferences to consume (Townsend 1988). There is positive, but not perfect, correlation in these shocks over time and over agents. Here all agents are risk averse (not just one of them as in the earlier example). However, shocks are private to only one agent at each date, and the identity of that agent alternates over time. That is, only one of the two parties in an initial period announces urgency today in the first period, hopefully compensated by more goods or value today if urgent, and the other, second party, announces tomorrow in the second period. The agents announce their states to the contract node, not to the other party, and then the smart-contract algorithm determines what is made public. This is where the optimal design kicks in.

If the announcement of the first agent in the first date were public, it would undercut insurance possibilities for the second date for the second agent. Typically, with allocations and histories of announcements known, there can be no insurance for the second agent in the second period. More is preferred to less, so it is hard to engineer an incentive-compatible trade-off

**Table 7.1**
Partitioned private ledgers and the gains from concealment.

Private information solution

| $\theta_0^a$ | $(c_0^a, c_0^b)$ | $\pi(c_0, \theta_0^a)$ | $\theta_0^a, \theta_1^b$ | $(c_1^a, c_1^b)$ | $\pi(c_1, \theta_1^b)$ |
|---|---|---|---|---|---|
| 0.2 | (1.75, 8.25) | 1.0 | (0.2, 0.2) | (4.75, 5.25) | 1.0 |
|  |  |  | (0.2, 0.9) | (2.0, 8.0) | 1.0 |
| 0.9 | $\begin{cases}(0.0, 10.0)\\(1.75, 8.25)\\(3.25, 6.75)\end{cases}$ | $\begin{cases}0.1159346\\0.0339681\\0.8544384\end{cases}$ | (0.9, 0.2) | (3.75, 6.25) | 1.0 |
|  |  |  | (0.9, 0.9) | $\begin{cases}(1.0, 9.0)\\(10.0, 0.0)\end{cases}$ | $\begin{cases}0.86106\\0.13839\end{cases}$ |

Agent $a$ has preference shocks, urgency to consume, $\theta_0^a$, at date $t=0$ of either 0.2 or 0.9. The announcement triggers consumption allocations $(c_0^a, c_0^b)$ for agents $a$ and $b$, the latter as the second party. These are listed in the second column of the table. Notice that if the announcement is 0.9, then a lottery puts about 3.3% probability on (1.75, 8.25) the deterministic allocation when 0.2 is announced. Probabilities $\pi(c_0, \theta_0^a)$ are in the third column of the table. At $t=1$, agent $b$ announces 0.2 or 0.9. The mechanism knows the previous history of incentive-compatible announcement of $\theta_0^a$ at $t=0$, but agent $b$ does not. The agent has an incentive to announce $\theta_1^b$ truthfully, and there is an insurance transfer along all paths. If, however, agent $b$ were to have seen $\theta_0^a$, there is no insurance over $\theta_1^b$ (top row right). Here, without that information, agent $b$ might be tempted to claim urgency, 0.9 always, but doing so risks losing everything with 14% probability if in fact agent $a$ had announced 0.9 (as in the bottom row, last column). In summary, when $(c_0^a, c_0^b) = (1.75, 8.25)$ is observed, agent $b$ remains uncertain of the type agent $a$ reported in $t=0$, and this is crucial for incentives.
*Source:* Townsend (1988).

other than a trivial one, no trade-off at all, to transfer a constant amount regardless of the state. However, if agent two in the second period were unsure of what was announced by agent one in the first period—something that a partitioned ledger can keep secret—then an optimized design will cause agent two to weigh the consequences of lying, announcing urgency but with positive probability ending up with very little consumption. Insurance and truth-telling are achieved by having the mechanism itself randomize over the consumption allocations in the first period as a function of agent one's message, so that actual allocations do not fully reveal either. That is, there are common elements in the support that can happen for any messages. Allocations are seen by all, but the message is not, and allocations do not reveal the whole story. With risk aversion, concave utility, this randomization *per se* comes with a welfare loss, but it is outweighed by the overall insurance benefit made possible by concealment. To summarize, agent two now faces a trade-off: If the agent announces a counterfactual state, succumbing to the temptation to lie, then with positive if small probability agent two would achieve a disastrous outcome.

We shall return to the discussion of randomization and concealment when we later address payments platforms.

## 7.2   Delegation of Portfolios to a Third Party: Platforms as Custodians

DLT allows commitment to a multiparty smart contract in which awards are allowed to vary over time as a function of shocks. When there are both private, unobserved idiosyncratic shocks and publicly observed aggregate shocks, it can make sense for households to delegate portfolio decisions and commit to a third-party custodian (Townsend 1988). This is a kind of endogenous centralization, with reliance on a third party, which is ironic given that those who promote distributed ledgers say that centralization is bad. This concentration of decision-making can happen in practice as with village funds, cooperatives, or wealth managers, or with exchange-traded funds that can be undone only by a restricted set of designated participants. But the decision of whether or not to do this is a function of the underlying environment, not an exogenous *desideratum*. The gain from a preprogrammed, third-party custodian is that it allows front-loading, as when incentive constraints in future periods bind, limiting the value of having resources then, so more value is paid out contemporaneously, or back-loading, which strengthens inter-temporal incentives by having more at stake in future periods contemporaneously as a function of what is said today.[1]

DLT can facilitate implementation of a multiparty contract with a commitment to the longer term, including sequestering funds to prevent withdrawal from the arrangement. The third-party custodian could appear as an implementing node, a financial institution, or a reserve bank, for example, engaged in a smart, multiparty contract.

## 7.3 Private vs. Public and the Role of Tokens

In this section we consider payment systems that are designed to be constrained optimal in support of trade, credit, and insurance.

The essential idea has been presented above several times: Distributed ledgers could keep track of messages as a part of the execution of a multi-period, multi-commodity, multi-agent smart contract and thus optimally allocate underlying risk, while facilitating trade and exchange.[2] Featured here in this section is the use of tokens, both single and multi-colored coins, to achieve this objective. The role of tokens is twofold. First, tokens are one way to interpret ledger entries in a centralized system, as colored entries. Second, tokens as real objects can allow a decentralized implementation of the same allocation, a hybrid system that can mitigate the scaling problems of centralized communication systems. If tokens are held in private, then incentives for voluntary disclosure need to be included, though this is not always a binding constraint. How well these various accounting and token systems function depends on the size of the message space relative to the needs for credit, insurance, and trade coming from the underlying economic environments. Nevertheless, in some instances, information should be kept private, so more limited message systems are actually preferred as constrained optimal.

### 7.3.1 Tokens on Ledgers as a Way to Achieve Unique Consensus; an Insurance Example with Voluntary Disclosure

As in Townsend (1987), suppose there are four agents in spatially separate locations and some subset of the agents travel. More specifically, a risk-averse agent $a$ is paired with a risk-neutral agent $b$ initially, in the first period at one of the two locations, such that the risk-neutral agent can insure the agent who is risk averse—and likewise, symmetrically, for agents $a'$ and $b'$ at a second location in the first period. If the pairings do not switch, we are back to the first example in chapter 6 on hybrid borrowing/lending and insurance pairwise.

But now suppose the pairings switch locations in the second period. Agents $a$ and $a'$ make announcements of their urgency to consume to their new partners, $b'$ and $b$, respectively. To induce truth-telling, if urgent in the first period, the agents receive the good but at the expense of getting less of it in the second period. Likewise, if patient today, the agent receives less of the good today at the benefit of getting more of it in the second period. A centralized public ledger for this four-agent, multiparty arrangement, which records all messages and keeps track of history, is one method of implementation. It reduces, equivalently, to the outcome of two separate pairings.

On the other extreme, if there were no record of announced preference shocks and no record of allocations in the first period, then there could be no link of the first period to the second period, and so, essentially, no insurance can be obtained in either period for agents $a$ and $a'$.

The introduction of tokens as a hybrid system can solve this problem without the centralization inherent in common ledgers. Announced patient agents in the first period receive more tokens than urgent agents. Tokens could be carried literally as coins or physical objects. In the second period, agents with more tokens can display them in order to be on the receiving end of goods. Tokens become the communication device and alleviate the burden of keeping track of history on a centralized ledger. Alternatively, consider private, immutable but partitioned ledger entries that are not validated by the entire community. Tokens or DLT entries are equivalent to each other; each conveys the necessary history.

### 7.3.2 Multiple Colored Tokens and Distinguished Histories: Trade with Insurance

We need not rely on pure insurance examples. In environments with two or more goods, there are exchanges of one good for another at each date, driven by the usual motives for spot trade, except those desires to trade are driven by preference shocks impacting inter-temporal trade-offs, and those are private.

Again, in a hybrid decentralized system, a portable, concealable token system could be used to keep track of trades in the first period. An agent may trade in the first period, give up one good and acquire the other, and be expected to reverse the situation in the future. This is the same patient urgent dichotomy but here for each good separately. That would be fine, as with the earlier examples; portable tokens can handle this situation. But now we introduce additional shocks to inter-temporal discount rates, with different shocks for different goods. After these shocks, agents may have ex post regrets and wish to reverse the trade in the first period in order to get the good they now most prefer in the second. One possible solution is to have multiple colored tokens, so as to have more dimensions in which to keep track of more detailed histories or, equivalently, multiple digital assets on a private ledger (see table 7.2).

These ideas in economics have tight links to cryptography and the idea of colored coins. The discussion here draws on Narayanan et al. (2016). As an example, ordinary Federal

**Table 7.2**
Colored coins and partitioned private ledgers.

| Multi-period private and full information solution, two goods | | | | | |
|---|---|---|---|---|---|
| Values for $(\theta_{1x}^a, \theta_{1y}^a)$ | $(c_x^a, c_y^a)$ | Values for $(\delta_x, \delta_y)$ | Values for $\theta_{2x}^a, \theta_{2y}^a$ | $(c_x^a, c_y^a)$ | |
| (.4, .6) | (2, 8) | (1, 1) | (.6, .4) | 8.01 | 2.0 |
| | | (.5, 1.5) | (.3, .6) | 1.0 | 8.0 |
| | | (1.5, .5) | (.9, .2) | 10.0 | 0.82 |
| (.6, .4) | (8, 2) | (1, 1) | (.4, .6) | 2.0 | 8.0 |
| | | (.5, 1.5) | (.2, .9) | 0.82 | 10.0 |
| | | (1.5, .5) | (.6, .3) | 8.0 | 1.0 |

Agent $a$ has utility function $U^a(c_x, c_y, \theta_1^a)$ at date $t=1$ over consumptions $c_x$ and $c_y$ with preference shocks $\theta_{1x}^a$ and $\theta_{1y}^a$, respectively. At date $t=2$, agent $a$ has utility $U^a(c_x, c_y, \theta_2^a)$. Note in particular the discount rate $\delta$ is random. Specifically, the utility function of agent $a$ at date 1 is of the form

$$U^a(c_x, c_y, \theta_1^a) = (c_x)^{\theta_{1x}^a} + (c_y)^{\theta_{1y}^a},$$

with $(\theta_{1x}^a, \theta_{1y}^a) \in \{(.4, .6), (.6, .4)\}$, each with equal probability, and at date 2 of the form

$$U^a(c_x, c_y, \theta_2^a) = (c_x)^{(1-\theta_{1x}^a)\delta_x} + (c_y)^{(1-\theta_{1y}^a)\delta_y}$$
$$= (c_x)^{\theta_{2x}^a} + (c_y)^{\theta_{2y}^a},$$

with

$$(\delta_x, \delta_y) = \begin{cases} (1, 1) & \text{with Prob } .96 \\ (.5, 1.5) & \text{with Prob } .02 \\ (1.5, .5) & \text{with Prob } .02 \end{cases}$$

Agent $b$ has linear preferences.

In the table, there are two goods, and agent $a$ can be a "borrower" or a "lender" in either good. Still, "preference reversal" shocks at date 2 can cause agent $a$ to want to pretend to have been a lender in the commodity the agent did not lend.
*Source:* Townsend (1987).

Reserve bank notes can be given bar codes so they can be used as purchased tickets to Yankee baseball games. The team signs a message that includes a specific game date, seat number, and serial number of the bill, with the signature of the issuer, all stamped on the bill. The advantage of using preexisting bank notes is that they cannot be easily counterfeited, so there would be no need to print new tickets. And such a system is decentralized. The message is written on the token, so to speak. Alternatively, the stadium could check a central database for information when a "ticketholder" enters the gate with a note having a certain serial number. The serial number links back to the primitive transaction, the purchase of the ticket. Either way, metadata is being attached to the note.

The point is that coins have publicly verified histories to trace ownership. This history can be made meaningful and put to other uses. Coins that "originate" in certain transactions can have associated extra metadata that behave like a color. The colors can also be considered as a metaphor, of course, as they could simply be bit strings. It is important, of course, that all participants understand the rules of this payment system so they know how to interpret the colors.[3]

To summarize simply, and to link back to the economics, distributed ledgers could keep track of messages as a part of the execution of a multi-period, multi-commodity, multi-agent smart contract, and thus optimally allocate underlying risk while facilitating trade and exchange. The "money" here, or more generally the payment system, is not separated from the motives for trade, intertemporal exchange, and insurance.

### 7.4 Permissioned Private Ledgers, When Consensus Is Not Unique Due to Optimally Kept Secrets

While multi-colored tokens convey more history, one should not jump to the conclusion that more information is preferred to less. We gave an example of private information and randomization earlier, with two agents, two dates, and one good. Shocks are private to only one agent at each date, and the identity of that agent alternates over time. If the announcement of the first agent in the first date were public, it would undercut insurance possibilities for the future.

If we generalize this example to four agents and imagine that agents cannot know what happened at the first date in a different location, then tokens can be allocated and tied to the random consumption allocation. Tokens can be carried into the second date, so the public part remains public. Yet tokens need not reveal entire histories of messages. That is, if tokens are colored data entries on private systems, there should not be unique consensus, in the words of Corda, in such environments.

The insurance example may seem a bit counterintuitive, but the same idea shows up in applied work in finance and with the same elements: risk aversion and information asymmetry. Lyon (1996) analyzes the optimal transparency of order-flow information as in foreign exchange markets, arguing that slower revelation of information—information that could reveal market-wide order flow—improves risk-sharing among dealers facing unavoidable position disturbances. Garratt et al. (2018) show in a similar but distinct context that some post-trade information disclosure can improve liquidity, but revelation of information (for sale) by a self-interested platform is a worse outcome than no information at all.

There are other examples of optimally limited shared information that make itineraries and validation endogenous. In Prescott and Townsend (2006b), auditors (or one might say validators) make incentive-compatible announcements of underlying states and then depart, making way for an incoming and relatively uninformed agent, assigned to be there as a solution to the mechanism design problem. The role of this auditor would be akin to verifying underlying states or objects on a ledger. For the incoming uninformed agents, they do not know what path they are on and face trade-offs, both in making announcements or in taking actions. Ironically, in this context, it is an advantage that past history is not known.

All these optimally designed systems require commitment to the design, including the control of information. Leakage is a potential problem in practice, and privacy remains a concern.

# 8
# Building Financial Infrastructure on Distributed Ledgers: Practical Application in Emerging Markets

## 8.1 Application: Building Financial Infrastructure in Developing Country Contexts

In this chapter, two sources are used to document that existing financial infrastructure is quite limited in developing countries. We feature an application in Southeast Asia (SEA) and Thailand in particular, then present examples of smart contracts that would help: escrow, letters of credit, waterfall payments, savings, insurance, and credit. A general equilibrium perspective on decentralized contract competition then follows, with an example of a proposed digital ledger technology (DLT) innovation.

## 8.2 Limited Financial Infrastructure

Banks in low-income and emerging market countries use legacy infrastructure. A large number of them do not deliver reliable, flexible banking solutions for low-income households and small and medium-sized enterprises (SMEs). According to a study commissioned by the Asian Development Bank on financial access and digital solutions, the percent of needs met by formal financial service providers in Indonesia, Philippines, Cambodia, and Myanmar ranges from 16–74% for savings, 48–72% for credit, 1–4% for insurance, and 11–35% for payments (Asian Development Bank 2017). The report also attaches US dollar estimates of these supply gaps, typically in the billions, and the percent that could be met with digital finance, which ranges from 19–44%.

It is not uncommon for households in SEA to be unable to access basic financial products or financial services critical to improving their standard of living. More than 70% of people living in Asia have no access at all to basic banking products such as bank loans. In some contexts, credit cards are not prevalent, and asset management services are rare indeed. While peer-to-peer lending services are emerging, the underlying custodian banking services are still lacking.

SMEs can only access a limited number of financial products, often at prohibitively high costs, even though SMEs constitute as much as 89–100% of all enterprises and account for 52–97% of total employment in countries that are part of the regional Association of Southeast Asian Nations (ASEAN 2017). SMEs are regularly credit-constrained, as financial institutions favor seemingly reputable and larger enterprises, such as those that are state-owned or owned by business magnates.

## 8.3 Analysis on the Ground: Townsend Thai Project

The Townsend Thai project (Townsend 2016), with its many years of collected data, allows for an in-depth study of financial access and informal markets. Overall, the sharing of risk so as to mitigate the impact of shocks onto consumption and production is good but not perfect. Idiosyncratic household and business-specific shocks are large and occur frequently; they constitute the bulk of the risk in a village economy. But notably, these idiosyncratic shocks are mostly, though not entirely, pooled away (Chiappori et al. 2014).

The mechanisms are local village or *tambon* (county) level "money markets." Households borrow to repay other preexisting loans and borrow to lend, making new loans; these behaviors are shown to be one source of consumption smoothing (Sripakdeevong and Townsend 2018). Delayed repayment on loans goes back through the credit chain, causing delays for those who have borrowed in order to lend. But early repayment also goes back through the credit chain, even more so quantitatively. Network maps trace out kinship and transaction-based links (Kinnan et al. 2018; Kinnan and Townsend 2012).

Within this scenario, one detects shortfalls and things not working well. Risk-sharing depends more on family/kin and how closely people are related in an ancestry tree. Trust may be an issue. Aggregate village-level or *tambon*-level shocks, by definition, are not diversifiable at the village level and, as confirmed in the data, end up in consumption. As in sophisticated financial markets, households with businesses running projects with self-financed or borrowed assets have rates of return that reflect those risk premia: Idiosyncratic shocks are largely pooled and have low-risk premia, and village-level aggregate shocks have higher-risk premia. But by the same standard, aggregate shocks across villages could be, but on average are not, pooled (Samphantharak and Townsend 2018). Thus there are geographic limitations.

### 8.3.1 Impact of Interventions: The Million Baht Fund with Scope for Improvement

In 2002, the government of Thailand set up a Million Baht Fund in every village, creating a quasi-formal, village-level institution run by local committee. Preexisting baseline and post-intervention panel data provide insights into how this influx of capital affected villages and households. Levels of consumption increased, among other variables (Kaboski and Townsend 2011, 2012). Investment and profits of those already in nonagricultural businesses increased if they had access to credit and productivity (Banerjee et al. 2018).

The informal sector acted as a catalyst, playing an augmenting, complementary role. For the relatively poor, the lowest-wealth quartile initially, the best-fitting financial regime shifted from a buffer-stock-saving regime to a costly-state-verification regime. In the latter, output levels can be claimed, but only claimed low outputs levels, which result in indemnities, are verified. This is a model of debt with contingencies. It is as if there were simple debt contracts with constant transfer back to investors, except that default with lower repayment is possible if underlying conditions are verified. Verification costs are shown to be lower when there are kinship households in the village (Ru and Townsend 2018).

But there is still room for improvement. Kinship ties can be a mixed blessing—what if no kin live nearby? Village fund committees did not allocate funds efficiently, as those who got loans were not found to have higher rates of return. The allocation was based more on family and political connections (Vera-Cossio 2018). Some of the village fund loan money did make its way indirectly to other households that were not engaged in direct borrowing, again through kin connections, as in the network credit chains. So this was helpful in mitigating efficiency losses. But it was not enough.

In summary, village funds, from this government program, did not reach, directly or indirectly, all of those who should have been ex ante optimal targets. The trust limitation of existing systems could be alleviated with DLT, as will be explained below. Improvement in existing systems is, of course, an implementation problem in its own right (Roth and Shorrer 2017). More work is needed on designs that will work in practice, in this context. Finally, there is relatively little financial infrastructure that works at the inter-village level.

## 8.4 Specific Examples of Smart Contracts

### 8.4.1 Collateral

As a lead example of conditionality and what is feasible with smart contracts on distributed ledgers, collateral can be put in escrow and released on certain verifiable conditions. This conditionality allows the use of tokens as collateral for loans, for example, but other assets can be used as well. Collateral in turn allows more distant parties who know little about one another to lend. There need be no trust *per se*.

### 8.4.2 Letters of Credit

De facto bank notes and letters of credit require not a bank *per se*, as with traditional and contemporaneous infrastructure, but only some third-party validation and/or novation. In a letter of guarantee, a third party underwrites the risk of the loan by providing escrow accounts of coins or other collateral that back the credit.

### 8.4.3 Waterfall Payment

This refers to agents who are linked to each other via economic transactions. For an example of what is possible for SMEs, receivable revenue can be contracted and secured in a trusted account. This can be used to buy inputs, for example. It could also be used to fund employee payroll. Employee accounts, when secured and sequestered, can be used in turn as collateral for borrowing. As another example, for village funds, the chains previously mentioned linking borrowing and repayment can be automated and, more to the point, extended beyond village boundaries. This can improve welfare relative to the currently used technology, which relies at best on promises, without a contracting technology that securitizes payment streams.

### 8.4.4 Savings Products

A simple savings product can also take advantage of conditionality. Thai households need to convert their cash to investments, as noted. This becomes a less acute problem when currency income is converted somehow to a coin/token in an e-wallet, because at that point, tokens can pay interest, and the opportunity cost of holding cash could be virtually zero. Still, one could then take the next step and create a portfolio management tool as a smart contract that either transfers funds automatically across accounts conditioned on states, according to some liquidity versus return trade-off, or uses an app that at least sends encrypted messages back to the saver as reminders. Brokers with algorithms could provide this service; if written up as smart contracts, then effectively the service is implemented on DLT.

Commitment savings could earn higher returns in tokens, paid into the wallet. Commitment accounts would be investments into escrow that limit withdrawals, if the savers wish to enter into these accounts. A predetermined quantity of tokens could be locked in a smart contract, which is programmed to release the tokens to the appropriate parties via airdrops when a set of conditions is met—for example, at the maturity date, after a lock-up period, or if certain programmed system conditions mandate a liquidity infusion.

### 8.4.5 Insurance

For community-level insurance, the initial contributions are prepaid premia into the mutual fund. Participants can choose among various options such as duration of the agreement, frequency and amounts of payments, and if/how to cash out. These are social rules that, when agreed on, become the smart contract.

For the payouts, the indemnities part of the community insurance, suppose a participant has low income, which could potentially be evident if, for example, wages are in coin. Then a simple conditional code will work well. To make the indemnity known to everyone in the fund, as the level of the remaining funds, with benefits, would be lower, there could be automated conditional messages to others, so as to achieve a public record of payouts. Messages are part of the distributed ledger and would be in sync; hence in the language of Corda there is a unique consensus. Another contingency: Low or ill-timed rainfall could be the source of low income, and rainfall is verified by sending a message to a data source, an oracle, and receiving a trusted message in return. The message, rainfall as a fact, is on the ledger and a key state variable. The oracle might need to be compensated.

With private information on income, an agent can send a message about the underlying situation, which could trigger an indemnity. The message could be published as in a database if these messages are to be public, though as discussed, optimal design of published data, conditionality, is not obvious. The optimal incentive-compatible messages for a contract can be found as the solution to a dynamic mechanism design problem. In equilibrium there is no problem with respect to what is reported by the agent because the agent, by design, has the right incentives, and at this point the code cannot be rewritten. The incentives come from a careful weighing of benefits versus costs as a function of outcome and reports, working out the optimal contracting part, putting the design into the smart contract and ledger. The presumption is that these improvements in insurance would outweigh costs of messages and memory.

### 8.4.6 Loans

With loans, an issue arises about how to grant them. One way to allow improved contracts is to allow other households to send messages about the underlying situation of that initial applicant agent. Studies have shown there is accurate information in the community on who should get loans, as some borrowers have higher expected returns (Hussam, Rigol, and Roth

2017). On the other hand, when households know that what they report has consequences for the initial would-be borrowing agent, who could be a friend or relative, then these other households are dishonest or even could collude in these reports. A possible solution is to pay for truthfulness using a peer-prediction index of subsequent events such as profits or repayment to the lender. This history of prediction performance in the past could be used for future rewards and penalties. While public reporting of messages alone appears to give households incentives to predict accurately, suffering loss of face for discrepancies between predicted and actual events, money or tokens might be able to do better to monetize loss of reputation. While some of these features are implemented in microcredit initiatives, they are far from universal and systematic. DLT provides a relatively inexpensive technology for implementation.

Multiple agents could also be sending reports simultaneously, as many contracts are multilateral. The design of the contract is such that each agent has an incentive to report truthfully if others are doing the same. A problem of collusion thus arises as noted: Agents coordinate in reports to get off-equilibrium beneficial outcomes. Yet, as noted earlier in Harris and Townsend (1981), the implementation literature provides insights on how to thwart this threat through multilateral conditionality. So, this too can be implemented as a smart contract.

In summary, distinguishing commodities and securities, points in time, and multiple agents, virtually any multiparty contract can be written as a smart contract.

## 8.5 The General Equilibrium Perspective on the Provision of Financial Services

Here we take a standard general equilibrium perspective, but with the inclusion of contracts. As noted in chapter 2, an economy consists of standard items, but with an innovation on the provision of financial services. The commodity space of a well-specified economy consists of factors of production such as land, labor, capital, and intermediate and final produced inputs and outputs, including capital and consumption goods. The commodity space also distinguishes time, as if there were time stamps; location, allowing for distinct geographies and shipping; and uncertainty, conditioning on states of the world, both exogenous and endogenous. Key actors are the users—that is, households and traditional firms. Some households run micro and small to medium-sized enterprises and are thus both households and firms combined. More generally, there is an ownership structure that specifies the shares that a household has in particular enterprises. An economy also specifies who knows what, at least initially, though signals can be generated, and some observe what others do or can make inferences. There are information partitions that capture these ideas.

The generalized commodity space becomes the space of incentive-compatible contracts written on top of the underlying traditional commodity space, but subject to contracting costs, as is enumerated below.

Efficiency of an economy is judged by the Pareto criterion. An allocation of feasible contracts is said to be efficient, or constrained-efficient, if there are underlying obstacles, if there does not exist an alternative feasible set of contracts that makes some households and firms better off and others no worse off. The current system, with its symptoms of limited access to financial products a priori, is inefficient in this sense.

We could go on to specify, as would be traditional, banks and markets as primitives of the economy, but it is here that we depart from the traditional model and break new ground. All possible forms of financial intermediation are on the table. Prescott and Townsend (1984a, 1984b) show how to decentralize such environments with a competitive broker-dealer sector for a multiplicity of information specifications. Prescott and Townsend (2006a) embed individual and multilateral contracts, as enumerated above, into an entire economy with a nexus of activities under contracts connected to general equilibrium flows. Competition among broker-dealers and intermediaries drives profits to zero, but these intermediaries remain essential for pooling, hence the language of disintermediation should not be used.

Relatedly, private information *per se* is not a rationale for regulation. Many economies decentralize in the sense of the welfare theorems. Joaquim, Townsend, and Zhorin (2018) model imperfect competition among financial service providers, including adverse selection. In this context, frictions interact with profits. Improved contracting technologies that do not also bring more entrants can decrease household and SME welfare.

## 8.6 Featured Example of Innovation: EvryNet

EvryNet is an intelligent financial automation operating system that aims to provide open-source banking services and financial contracts to unbanked and underbanked populations. It is being built on the need-smart-contract premise and incorporates the general equilibrium perspective. The system is still under development as of this writing.

EvryNet is creating an interoperable smart-contract platform that enables not only traditional banks but also microfinance institutions and others to initiate and execute banking products and financial contracts. The envisioned provision of contracts should be at competitive prices because of competition across providers in the provision of computer memory (storage) and computation power. A rating system tracks performance of providers in validation.

The financial services consist of a multitiered architecture. The core component of the platform is a financial service portal that users and institutions can utilize to draft financial contracts, either standard or customized. The portal is underpinned by a smart-contract composer, which enables smart-contract creation using DLT. Once the user selects a smart-contract template, specifies necessary inputs, and selects nodes based on trust or reputation score, the smart contract will be processed through EvryNet's virtual machine.

The smart contract can optionally check for compliance or necessary regulations. For instance, the EvryNet platform can allow the relevant organizations to certify by signing the contract digitally or even by executing the compliance-check code to ensure regulation compliance. It allows event-hooking in smart contracts to seamlessly receive relevant events from external entities. Many real-world smart contracts may need external inputs to complete the conditional transactions—for example, the confirmation of a shipment.

In summary, rather than take as given the current set of institutions and markets, often sparse, the vision of EvryNet is to re-create them through the new, distributed ledger contract technologies, including executing nodes as a new production section. However, the costs of coding, validating, and provisioning memory for optimal contract design could, as noted earlier, impact contract design and/or have implications for validation systems and the degree of decentralization.

# 9
# Payment Systems on Distributed Ledgers: Practical Applications

We now present two designs for payment systems that use distributed ledgers. One such was implemented by the Bank of Canada for commercial banks for use in the interbank market, Project Jasper. This design is largely about the potential to improve on existing systems or at least validate that DLT payments can do as well as traditional systems. Initially with Ethereum, and then subsequently with Corda, the project was ultimately successful, including time lockups in a multilateral queuing system.

A second system is under development in Southeast Asia for money transfer operators who engage in the Lightnet international fiat money exchange, with Lightnet transferring fiat tokens across boundaries. This design is about creating and implementing something new and can include ultimately constrained-optimal designs for trade, credit, and insurance in coordination with a digital reserve system.

## 9.1  Interbank Payments: Project Jasper

To summarize from the Payments Canada (2017) white paper, Project Jasper is an experiment in private permissioned distributed ledgers that allows for the exchange of central-bank-issued digital assets. The goal is to transform the payment structure in Canada. If an improved ecosystem could be built, there could be significant benefits for the whole financial sector and the economy overall. It is important to keep pace with the shift to digital commerce and remove impediments and to try to get as close as possible to a frictionless end-to-end customer experience. In experimental simulations, Project Jasper could indeed handle the high volume of Canada's large-value interbank transfer system.

Project Jasper first explored Ethereum and then moved to R3's Corda platform to allow for improvements in settlement finality, scalability, and privacy. As noted in the white paper, DLT allows improved back-office payment processing and reconciliation with and across participating financial institutions, reducing the likelihood of costly errors and improved automation through the use of smart contracts.[1] Another goal of Project Jasper was cybersecurity, creating backup ledgers to eliminate single points of failure.

As noted in the Payments Canada white paper as well, it is possible to limit information on a database when privacy and confidentiality concerns among parties are paramount. For example, in Project Jasper, parties see only their own activity. The role of the Corda notary node is played by the Bank of Canada, though Corda can eliminate the need for such a single trusted database operator.

Netting promotes funding efficiency and smoother intraday-payments flow. Phase 2 of Project Jasper appears to be one of the first instances of a central queue within a DLT platform for payments. For example, a participant's account gives permission for a bounded, specified amount of value to be placed into a queuing option. This can be changed, but not when the queuing algorithm is running; during that time the participant is blocked as codes search over best transfers.[2] Phase 3 extended the phase 2 proof of concept to the settlement of exchange traded equities.

The central bank maintains a commitment to settle accounts but has risk exposure in doing so, and so collateral is posted by participants. Technically, in Jasper there are two versions that differ in the collateral and loss allocation procedures: The defaulter pays, and the survivors pay through pooled risk.[3]

Project Jasper is illustrative of sophisticated multiparty smart contracts used in the design of a payment system, showing what is feasible to do with distributed ledger technology. Other potential examples of DLT-based payment systems come from the Monetary Authority of Singapore. Nevertheless, there is some skepticism among central bankers concerning DLT interbank systems for large-value payments. Are they really needed? The Project Jasper application succeeded in re-creating the functionality of an existing traditional payment infrastructure—that is, on one hand, it did as well, but on the other hand it did not dominate.

Still one does wonder if the reconciliation, data security, and contract commitment advantages of DLT are being under-emphasized in the attempt to replicate existing systems.

The Project Jasper white paper does note, in addition, that DLT is particularly relevant, likely needed for cross-border payments. Current infrastructure still relies on financial institutions maintaining their own databases, and so counterparty risk is high. Subsequent collaboration among the Bank of England, the Bank of Canada, and the Monetary Authority of Singapore has explored in detail the limits of current interbank transfer systems and the possible use of distributed ledger technology (see Kimberley 2019; also Monetary Authority of Singapore 2018).

## 9.2 Optimized Design of Cross-border Payments: Lightnet and Velo

Consider the case of Cambodian or Myanmar migrants in Thailand, migrants who both need to fund their trip (now regulated) and to send money back home to family. Remittances in Southeast Asia amounted to $63.9 billion in 2016, while over the six years leading up to 2016, transfer fees grew by 3% to 7.1% (Leong 2017). The high transfer fees are partly a result of legacy technology in the formal sector and limited access to formal currency exchange markets. Traditionally, a money transfer operator (MTO) conducts cross-border transactions using a single server to record transactions among its international subsidiaries, going through traditional financial institutions or entering into a bilateral agreement with an MTO in another country. This limits the number of partners a given MTO can have and results in high transaction costs.

Lightnet proposes to create for MTOs in Southeast Asia a highly liquid decentralized settlement layer on a permissioned blockchain. It is a hybrid in the sense that it uses, and effectively transfers, fiat money. It does this with its own fiat tokens that have been minted by posting collateral tokens (Velo) to the Velo protocol. MTOs can be viewed as agents with varying underlying balance sheets hit by the needs of their customers for trade.

To trace out a sample transaction, a client, to be called Alan, asks an MTO in Thailand to transfer money to Alice in Cambodia. Alan is essentially lending money as a deposit to the Thai MTO, which will be extinguished when Alice in Cambodia receives her money. We come to the determination of the exchange rate (as discussed below). At some point in the time line, Alice receives a text message that her money from Alan is in. Alice then goes to a payment gateway—for example, a 7-Eleven or a registered point-of-sale (POS) store—and shows a QR code from the text message. The 7-Eleven staff scans it and gives Alice the money. At this point, the Cambodian MTO is lending money to the Thai MTO. Conceptually this is to be repaid, ideally, by a transaction in the reverse direction. More generally, though, netted transactions among a larger community of MTO operators happen in a multilateral clearing operation. We come back to this later.

When the Thai MTO first enters Lightnet, it enters into a smart contract and converts Thai fiat money into Thai baht collateral. In return for its deposit, the MTO gets an intraday Thai fiat credit balance in Thai fiat tokens. This serves as an upper bound for outgoing remittance transactions on any given day. During the day, the Thai MTO then initiates the transaction for Alan by submitting the order to Lightnet, giving up some of its Thai baht credit line. In turn, Lightnet posts collateral for it Thai fiat accounts, secured as backed by Velo tokens. These tokens are acquired as a loan from Velo labs or a grant (or purchased on an exchange, which we will come back to).

Lightnet maintains an off-chain order book, linked to Stellar. When initiating the transaction, Alan's Thai MTO queries the Lightnet order book and finds the best offer exchange rate, asking Alan whether he wants to continue (Alan could withdraw at that point). The order book matches MTO orders on behalf of customers to funding from liquidity providers (not simply banks but others, arguably with lower cost of funds). In the case of the Alan-Alice example transaction, the liquidity provider is giving up Cambodian riel. Such transactions are grouped and offset before sending batched orders to Stellar at regular intervals. Order-book matching maintains an accurate source of transactional reference between any two transacting MTOs, providing reconciliation. This reduces the probability of disputes and delays, a feature of DLT commented on earlier in chapter 3. The Lightnet settlement network and the Velo protocol are built on Stellar, which provides interoperability. Velo hopes to achieve a transaction throughput of 1,000+ per second, with each transaction taking three to five seconds at a very low cost, a tiny fraction of a penny.

At the end of the day, as anticipated, the many transactions that occur among all MTOs will be netted using a digital reserve system's distributed ledger algorithm. Each MTO will be notified about how much it needs in order to settle its credit line. If the MTO successfully settles its end-of-day balance, its fiat credit balances will be replenished, also resulting in an increase in the MTO's credit rating. Alternatively, if any MTO fails to settle the balance, the MTO's fiat collateral will be liquidated, which had been locked as collateral, executing the conditionality of the contract and cutting the MTO's credit rating.[4] Under this system, counterparties can conduct transactions with multiple pairings in different countries without having to trust each other.

Some MTOs are already engaged in contractual bilateral relationships, with fiat credit and e-credit lines. In principle, depending on these relationships, they handle credit and insurance with each other. This was noted in chapter 4 on M-Pesa and in Indonesia. Going one step further, the implementation of constrained-optimal contracts among MTOs is possible. This could be implemented on DLT as envisioned in the examples on information-constrained credit and insurance in chapter 7.

# 10
# Regulation and the Use of Distributed Ledger Technology

In this chapter we group together various insights from theory that pertain to optimal regulation of financial systems. In several cases, distributed ledger technology can play a central role in mitigation of bank and market runs and in coordinating payment devices related to the issue of digital assets, for instance. More generally, free and open competition as in the EvryNet platform can suffer from coordination problems, especially under traditional regulation. Market structure and its regulation needs to be part of the overall ex ante design.

## 10.1 Mitigating Runs on Banks and Markets

DLT can improve on current technology used by banks and markets in order to mitigate resulting runs. Diamond and Dybvig (1983) wrote a seminal paper on bank runs. The idea is that investors deposit their funds in a bank. The bank can invest in a short-term asset or tie up funds with a longer-term investment. Yet depositors retain the option of withdrawing funds early, which they would like to do if they are hit with a preference or other shock that makes it more urgent to have the funds. Ideally, the bank could plan on the fractions of agents in the population who will be urgent (or the opposite, more patient) and invest accordingly. However, if more than that fraction of urgent households gets the idea there is a run on the bank, then patient investors, fearing a disproportionate number will withdraw early, leaving little for the longer term, will run also. The point is that this can become a self-fulling prophesy, a valid if horrible equilibrium. There is a more recent literature on market runs rather than bank runs that draws an analogy (Martin, Skeie, and von Thadden 2013, 2014) so that the logic of runs applies beyond banks.

Though mitigation of runs is an important rationale for intervention, as in deposit insurance, that can bring other distortions, no market discipline on the bank means regulators must take on even more responsibility for what the bank might be doing. Indeed, the monetary authority may have to inject liquidity if banks have taken on too much risk and investments go bad, and banks' anticipating this action exacerbates the problem.

Yet the problem of runs has a partial if not complete solution that can be found within the mechanism design literature itself. A simple version is suspended convertibility, thus reassuring investors that some of their money would remain, regardless. More sophisticated, sequential-service models treat customers differently depending on when they arrive at the trading window—that is, on the history of traders and trades before them, determining their incentives to announce privately observed shocks (Green and Lin 2003).

This is where distributed ledgers can play a key role. Messages in distributed ledgers are essentially time-stamped and immutable, so it is quite natural to think about history based on previous reported transactions in the blockchain as being used to determine consequences for contemporary actions and messages. With independent private values, there is a unique Bayesian Nash equilibrium that eliminates runs entirely and is a dominant strategy equilibrium. Thus multiple equilibria, as in the original Diamond-Dybvig model, is no longer a problem. With correlated private values, some run-like phenomena remain, as the history of traders at any moment in time is, on the one hand, self-reported and yet, on the other, desired as a key statistic, as it is revealing of aggregates. Nevertheless, the risk of runs can be substantially mitigated.

These mechanisms could be used in practice as a private-sector alternative to public liquidity. This could dramatically mitigate the central bank moral-hazard problem, that bailouts ex post create perverse private-sector incentives ex ante. This could also alleviate the concern that private platforms might somehow pose a systemic risk. They can be designed to guard against that. Optimal regulation would then amount to verifying that the platforms that implement these insights are designed properly.

Here, of course, there is a political economy issue. Getting diverse parties to agree to these changes is nontrivial, especially if banks benefit from government largess. Another qualification stems from the latency in networks, which confounds the chronological ordering. A modification of the model to treat identically a set of orders that are received over small intervals of time will need to be designed. Budish, Cramton, and Shim (2015) propose such a mechanism to deal with high-frequency traders. Likewise, a related finance literature outlines the trade-offs between frequency of adjustment and thick markets (Du and Zhu 2017).

## 10.2 The Limits of Competition for Contracts: Coordination and Re-optimized Regulation

It was argued earlier in chapter 8 that when smart contracts are needed, one can envision competition among intermediaries in offering such contracts, consistent with a Walrasian equilibrium, with its Pareto optimality properties. There are, however, caveats and advice to regulators that come from general equilibrium theory. Specifically, following Pesendorfer (1995) and Makowski (1980), one can begin in an economy with incomplete markets and contracts and then allow financial service providers to innovate. One might hope this would complete the markets, but it may not, because of complementarities in uncoordinated innovation. More coordination would be needed. A related point: Ill-informed or outdated regulation can segment an industry and make the needed coordination impossible.

In addition, markets and access should not be entirely open all the time to anyone. When there is private information and minimal scales of operation, then some forms of competition can undercut incentives and optimal diversification. Equity markets should not free-ride on existing infrastructure, for example. Certain kinds of exclusivity are needed. Competition should be ex ante for the right to provide services, not ex post to draw off customers from contracts. As in Acemoglu and Zilibotti (1997), minimum scales of operation across sectors means that risk-sharing is incomplete. Stretching the extensive margin to high minimum-scale projects is good, but this means less funding for each active project; on the margin some high-scale projects receive at the optimum relatively more funding than other zero or lower-end projects, as the resources must come from somewhere. The point: Portfolios are not balanced in funding. Unrestricted trade into equities issued by firms would undercut the optimum; investors will want to diversify their eggs into the various baskets equally. Instead, one intermediary should do all the packaging. There can be ex ante competition for this right. Townsend and Xandri (2018) provide blueprints for market design and regulation in this context.

Retrading among potential deposits in the Diamond-Dybvig model (1983), as in Jacklin (1987), is another negative factor. Retrading undercuts the implicit provision of insurance for the impatient. Distributed ledgers with ex ante contracts and commitment to market structure can prevent this from occurring.

Blueprints for the ultimate design are needed, as otherwise the system experiencing innovations may develop piecemeal and not achieve a constrained-efficient outcome. Regulators need to see the blueprints and understand the big picture.

## 10.3 Lessons from Monetary Theory for the Regulation of Payment Systems: The Need for Coordination

Lack of key common information may make it difficult to achieve optimal targets and, further, can lead to market crashes. Thus there are clear implications for micro/macroprudential regulation. Ironically, DLT, rather than being a regulatory concern, offers an obvious solution in the context of these problems.

### 10.3.1 The Impossibility of Decentralized Exchange

A natural objective is to try to achieve the Pareto optimal allocation associated with a Walrasian competitive equilibrium. Ostroy and Starr (1974) ask whether this can be done under a decentralized exchange when information is limited, or rather, whether centralization of some information is necessary.

These problems emerge despite the fact that in the Ostroy and Starr (1974) model, many important items are simply taken as given, so that there are as few obstacles as possible. The target Walrasian allocation is given; the prices as common marginal rates of substitution in the Walrasian allocation are given and fixed; and paths over time of matched agents are known in advance. Furthermore, agents simply act as computers implementing code. Here is the question: How do you write the code to implement this targeted social optimum? The answer: It is impossible to always do this when information is decentralized. The key insight: Information on the distributed ledger should be public in some clearly delineated instances.

In the Ostroy-Starr model, money plays the role of unit of account. There are potentially many agents and many underlying commodities. Agents start out in the model with underlying endowments of commodities. But the model would apply equally well to endowments of securities, various possible fiat monies, or combinations of all these. Actual payment systems handle retail and wholesale trade, securities settlement, and cross-border currency flows.

Agents in the model meet pairwise and then trade. The point is that not everyone is together all the time in one spot—they are matched, for example, in an over-the-counter (OTC) market. Trade in the model is monetized as a payment order in a *quid pro quo* condition: When goods are supplied, the supplier is given unit of account credits, in monetary terms. Likewise, when goods are purchased, the purchaser is assigned debits in the unit of account, in monetary terms. Under a natural *quid pro quo* spot-trade condition, the value of the purchases must match the value of sales in each and every contemporary bilateral transaction. Here, then, there is no credit. The prices used to value commodities and securities come from the target Walrasian allocation (known). Indeed, the entire point is to try to achieve the Walrasian allocation in a decentralized way.

Transaction values are placed on the ledgers as flows as they occur, and this results in new commodity/asset positions as stocks. Of course, as emphasized from the outset of this book and from the discussion of accounts and ledgers in chapter 8, the corresponding trade ledgers (flow) and asset ledgers (change in stocks) must be consistent.

In a key example provided by Ostroy and Starr (1974) and a technical correction by Kim (2015), it is shown that the appropriate trades across agents when they meet in subsets can require centralized knowledge of the underlying environment and trade histories. In particular, knowledge of identities of agents, histories of trade, and initial excess demands are needed, not only pairwise of those contemporaneously matched, but also of others with whom the contemporaneous set of matched traders has not been matched previously. The idea is straightforward: Implementation is both forward- and backward-looking. One has to know where the system should be headed, the target, and the remaining options in the future to reach that target, hence what trades need to have been accomplished in the past in order to make this feasible. Sometimes there are multiple choices of trades to make and more than one way to do things within a given contemporaneous pairing. Guidance is needed, from the forward and backward perspective. However, not all past histories are crucial; in the key example, there is only one instance in which information would need to be shared.

In the Ostroy-Starr (1974) and Kim (2015) example, private information about initial excess demand is the source of the potential problem. However, one can think of some initial trading period appended onto the beginning of the Ostroy-Starr model, differing from the Ostroy-Starr initial period—perhaps earlier trading rounds that determine excess demand at the time we tune into the Ostroy-Starr initial period. These initial excess demands are the deviations remaining from the ultimate target. If there were a common-consensus verified ledger to which all traders had access, then this required information would be known.

Ostroy and Starr (1974) do also discuss alternatives that mitigate the need for centralized common information. They describe what could be termed a *monetary solution*, sufficient ex ante liquidity in one of the commodities, termed the *money good*, ample enough so that expenditures of commodities or asset purchases of any agent can be financed out of this liquidity, regardless of who meets whom when and regardless of underlying economy-wide efficient targets for trade. But that amount of liquidity, whether a commodity or fiat money or tokens, is large and potentially costly, as liquidity held for this purpose is not invested in economic activities. This is made more explicit in other models.[1] Real-time gross settlement systems are in fact frequently run as hybrids with liquidity-saving mechanisms made possible by computer algorithms and queues (Martin and McAndrews 2008).

Another Ostroy-Starr alternative is a central warehouse, such as a very large broker-dealer with whom all can trade, though such a large entity could bring other distortions—namely, market power. A third alternative is credit, as if from a Walrasian banker, of the kind witnessed in early trade fairs (Townsend 1990). In the Ostroy-Starr model, however, this requires two more rounds of trade at the beginning and end: to get the credit, then the featured round of trading, and then repayment. In their model, this violates the desired criterion to achieve all trade in one round of pairings only.

It is tempting to think of the Walrasian banker as a central bank or digital reserve bank. In practice, for good reasons, central banks worry about intraday exposure and thus require good collateral. In the spirit of Ostroy-Starr, but going beyond the model, central banks also worry about the ultimate motive for trades, such as interbank borrowing transactions that are passing through their payment system but are not designated as such. Central banks would like to know more about what is driving transactions, given macroprudential concerns.

### 10.3.2 Information Problem with Private Monies: Circulating Private Debt and Multiple Media of Exchange Equilibria

A somewhat related setting is found in Townsend and Wallace (1987), who focus on payments made via high-velocity privately issued debt. Securities can serve as payment devices and circulate (remember the English tally sticks of chapter 5). The point here is that this is an issue with e-securities or e-assets. E-tokens are designed to facilitate liquidity and trade, but there can be problems.

The idea that securities can serve as payment devices should be familiar. In New York markets, for example, brokers experience shortages of various securities. Under rehypothecation of collateral, a lender who gives up cash for securities as collateral becomes a borrower in turn, passing the collateral on along a chain. Singh (2011) finds the velocity of circulation of treasuries is now higher than the standard monetary aggregate (M2). This can compete with fiat currency, as in Muley (2016). Carlson et al. (2016), Greenwood, Hanson, and Stein (2016), Krishnamurthy and Vissing-Jorgensen (2012), and others are all consistent in finding a liquidity premium for those treasuries. On-the-run treasuries have become money-like assets, one might say more like money than money itself. This has policy implications, clearly, though exactly what to do about it depends on the point of view of the analyst.

Table 10.1 from Townsend and Wallace (1987) provides an instructive example environment. There are four agents, four periods, and two locations. Agents have endowments of a consumption good that varies over time, but again, as earlier, one can generalize and imagine these are other objects such as securities. One can trace out chains of named debt from the issuer at the issue date passing through third parties to the issuer at the redemption date (here no reneging is allowed). This circulating private debt is the medium of exchange in contemporaneous transactions, supporting trade in other short-term noncirculating securities and the consumption commodity. One can take the consumption good as the numeraire, but again, as earlier, the idea can be generalized.

The point of the model is that there is a coordination problem. There are many potential equilibria, each of which achieves the same target Pareto optimal allocation, the complete-markets equilibrium real allocation. But these equilibria vary in who is issuing the debt initially and hence what objects are circulating—that is, what objects are serving as payment

**Table 10.1**
Circulating private debt: who meets whom when.

| | Location | |
|---|---|---|
| Date | 1 | 2 |
| 1 | (1,2) | (3,4) |
| 2 | (1,3) | (2,4) |
| 3 | (1,2) | (3,4) |
| 4 | (1,3) | (2,4) |

This illustrative table has four traders. Agent 1 is always at location 1 and agent 4 is always at location 2. Agents 2 and 3 alternate locations. There is scope for bilateral borrowing at dates 1,3 and 2,4 as the same agents are paired. There is also scope for circulating debt through chains of pairings—for example, an IOU issued by agent 1 at $t=1$ is passed to agent 2, who in turn presents it to 4 at $t=2$, who passes it to 3 at $t=3$, with redemption by the issuer, agent 1 at $t=4$. There are many other feasible circulating debt chains.
*Source:* Townsend and Wallace (1987).

devices. In a key example, to be specific, agents 1 and 2 are matched in location one, and agents 3 and 4 are matched at location two. Agents 1 and 4 stay put at their respective locations, but agents 2 and 3 keep switching back and forth across locations from one period to the next. Again, there are many equilibria that achieve the Pareto optimal target: Either all the debts that are allowed to circulate could be issued by initial parties in the first of the two locations, or by the parties in the other, second location, or they could be issued in various particular convex combinations. But by assumption, in the informationally decentralized market environment, there is no way for traders in one location to know what is going on in the other. Too much or too little debt as liquidity could be issued.

This can cause problems later in subsequent markets. Some circulating debts would be "overissued," resulting in a precipitous drop in their prices later on in the trading cycle. Agent-traders would suffer from unnecessary excessive fluctuations in their intertemporal consumption profile. Interestingly, the drop does not happen right away, as trade in short-term assets in early periods after the mismatch is discovered can partially compensate. Eventually some, but not all, parties along the transaction chains suffer drops in consumption—namely, those carrying the circulating debt across locations (Spector and Townsend 2019). Failure to achieve coordination can link up with observed chaotic conditions. Bills of exchange were traded in the London money markets, and these crashed, leading to arguments for the creation of a central bank.

DLT keeping track and verifying initial issues of long-term money-like debt in exchange for consumption or other objects, if public, would achieve in the example environment the necessary coordination. A related point: Not all information need be shared all the time. Here it is only information on initial security issues. Interestingly, and a warning to policymakers, there are no liquidity premia associated with the circulating private debt to be discerned from the data, yet the coordination problem remains. The crash comes as a surprise. The lesson for policymakers: A clear understanding of the environment and consequent tracking of transactions data is needed.

# 11
# Cryptocurrency: The Role and Value of Tokens in Economies with Distributed Ledger Systems

This chapter focuses on tokens and cryptocurrency, reviewing the velocity and frequency of use in payment definitions of money and the prevalence of multiple media of exchange in many economies, including monies indirectly backed. One implication of mechanism design theory pinpoints the special role of tokens relative to fiat money fungibility: Unrestricted use of fiat money hurts implementation. Implications from monetary theory for valued fiat money are reviewed, distinguishing two branches: one in which for various models the value of money is endogenous, and potentially indeterminate, and another in which money has a value for sure, because of taxes or legal stipulations. But regardless of what gives fiat monies value, tokens in hybrid systems can play a role and have value, built on top of the fiat structure, when there are sufficient gaps without them. Indeterminacy in token values in this context has remedies in the same roots of monetary theory: interest and use requirements. Smart contracts can implement these remedies. Relatedly, a digital reserve system can implement activist token policies armed with transactions data from the distributed ledger. The ideas for doing so come from the various monetary models, with their explicit micro underpinnings. But to reiterate, these digital token policies are recommended even when the rest of the economy is monetized with valued fiat money, as tokens can be a complement and deal optimally with the gaps that remain.

Various points of clarification concerning tokens are worth making at the outset, one to reiterate and others that have been only implicit thus far. First, tokens and cryptocurrency are not a necessary part of distributed ledgers. Digital Asset does not use coins in their implementations in the Australian stock market; the same is true for ledgers in land titles, Walmart's tracking system, and Maersk's shipping logistics. Second, even if there were tokens in any one of these or other systems, this *per se* should not be surprising given the multiplicity of monies we see in practice in many economies. The appearance of a token does not mean that it *per se* has to compete with fiat currency. Third, a token can be used not only as a valued means of payment like a currency, but also as a utility token, necessary for purchasing goods or services with the cryptocurrency company or platform. Fourth but separate, a token may originate with an initial coin offering as a fund-raising device. The latter may sound suspicious, but Garratt et al. (2018) delineate potential advantages in an economic model. Fifth, tokens are also associated with tokenized securities. In this chapter, we are primarily concerned with tokens as a means of payment and as a utility coin, and not the other issues.

To begin, this chapter reviews definitions of money and then reviews the implications of mechanism design for the relationship of tokens to fiat money; uncontrolled use of the latter can undercut the incentives of the former. There follows a review of the implications of monetary theory, not simply for fiat money, but also for the role of tokens in hybrid systems, regardless of what is giving fiat monies their underlying value. Implications for the indeterminacy of token values and the divergence of private and social values are reviewed, as evidenced in the loss of the fundamental welfare theorems, with empirical tests. Remedies for indeterminacy are given, as implemented in an envisioned innovation with money transfer operators in Southeast Asia. Finally, optimal activist token policies come from monetary models combined with data from transactions on distributed ledgers, gathered as part of intrinsic operations of the envisioned digital reserve system.

## 11.1  Media of Exchange, Definitions of Money

Bech and Garratt (2017) display as a taxonomy flower the various kinds of money in existence. For us here, rather than stress a distinction between fiat money versus cryptocurrency, as if there were room for only one or the other, likewise for outside money versus private credit, we can adopt standard definitions and turn to data for measurement. This provides an impartial and unitary treatment of what we mean by money— simply something used frequently in transactions. The conclusion is that, even within a given economy, there are multiple media of exchange, and so we would not be surprised to find that tokens of various kinds, depending on the purposes, can play complementary roles.

The standard definitions have to do with velocity and frequency of use in payment. *Velocity* of an object is the average amount traded per unit of time divided by the stock outstanding. The velocity of fiat money is a key object, though alternative measures of the stock run from base money, M0, to larger aggregates including commercial banks deposits, M1, M2, and so on.

A payment matrix enumerates in its rows and columns what is exchanged for what. An object in a given row may have a high proportion of value in use to acquire several other objects specified in each of the columns. If the numbers are high, then such an object can be called money. Within a given economy, multiple devices can be used, in addition to the associated country's fiat money. The extent of this varies across economies, but multiplicity is not uncommon.

## 11.2 Multiple Media Are Typical

In contrast to thinking of fiat currency or Bitcoin as competing entities, a payments matrix for ICRISAT village economies in India shows prevalent use of both grain and fiat currency (rupees) (Lim and Townsend 1998). Grain is used to pay labor, for example. In country-level economies with advanced payment systems, such as the United States, household surveys from the Federal Reserve Bank of Boston show the use of fiat money currency but also the use of checks, debit, and credit cards (Bitcoin is negligible so far) (Schuh and Stavins 2014). A related point: A given agent typically uses multiple media over relatively short periods of time, though different agents use different subsets.

Of course, an object, good, or security can be useful and have value, even if it has low velocity. Relatedly, we often see layering, with some payment devices backed by others. Some systems operate offline. The indirect claims can have high velocity, while the underlying backing need not. Fiat money, for example, is relatively recent. Previously, government monies were backed by gold (or silver), and in principle, gold certificates as government bank liabilities could be redeemed. It was simply easier to trade paper claims than cash in and transport the gold that otherwise was held in depositories. Currently, commercial banks are required to hold some central bank reserves, hence to hold fiat money. In turn, banks issue claims such as demand deposits so that, again, payment devices are indirectly backed. Likewise, tokenized securities are sometimes created with the express purpose of generating liquidity, deeper and more accessible markets to transfer claims.

Private debt can also be money in a given economy, an asset with high velocity. Suppose that agents trust the entity issuing the liability to always honor redemptions even when presented by third parties. In economic terminology, there is full commitment on the part of the issuer to repay at full face value. Paper checks are written instructions by a customer to its trusted banker to transfer value to a third party. Countersigned, postdated checks circulated as money in Paraguay when the penalty for overdrawing was prison. Historically, bills of exchange drawn on the issuer have circulated as media of exchange. Trade credit can also act as liquidity (Amberg et al. 2016). Tally sticks were mentioned earlier in chapter 5 on encryption.

Nowadays, fiat tokens are a leading example relevant to the discussion here. They represent a combination of public and private monies backed by trust. A named trusted entity in Stellar acts as an anchor. A customer deposits an amount of fiat money with the anchor, either paper currency or a claim on another commercial bank. The anchor issues the customer an IOU for the deposit. The anchor then issues a token, which is a claim on that fiat deposit. These tokens go on to be traded in the Stellar marketplace through the order books of broker-dealers. This was implicit in the discussion of Stellar under cryptography in chapter 5 (section 5.5.3). These fiat tokens could have high velocity, as when they are cashed in quickly. For example, flows come back the other way from the country of destination to the country of origin, balancing the original transaction, giving another customer ownership of the fiat deposit.

If there is something special about cryptocurrencies, it is the irony that they are at risk of functioning *too well* as a means of payment, with almost costless creation, execution, and extinction. The costs are low and, in some cases, interconnectedness is high, so one can get into and out of coins almost instantaneously. In principle, we get close to a world without frictions in which, at most, tokens become a unit of account. With no one holding the coin, the value is not pinned down. That is, as a unit of account, transactions can be denominated in tokens, but this is an arbitrary convention and does not pin down values *per se*—or better put, the value is pinned down by fixing the unit of account measures, a par value, not by the underlying economics.

There is nothing odd or new here. We know from basic Walrasian theory for competitive markets that the unit of account is arbitrary. Furthermore, pure accounting systems can clear markets with sequential or delayed payment, allowing purchases of commodities and securities before sales. This unit of account role of money has been displayed historically in trade fairs and the prevalence of ghost currencies (Cipolla 1956; Townsend 1990). Despite sequential trade in goods and the presence of banks, little actual coin was used in trade or deposited into accounts. Revealingly, accounts could be kept in defunct, devalued coinage. Money transfer ledger systems among sitting local bankers were prevalent in early medieval Europe (McAndrews and Roberds 1999).

## 11.3 Lessons from Mechanism Design for Tokens

In some economic environments, tokens can increase trade and welfare, as in the earlier sections of chapter 4, where we noted the role that tokens can play in implementation of the solution to mechanism design problems, either as physical coins or as information partitions. Furthermore, multiple colored tokens can be used in some economic environments so that there would be a welfare loss from collapsing to one. Kocherlakota (1998) makes the same point in a different way: He emphasizes that (a single) money serves only as partial memory.

Relatedly, in mechanism design, unobserved actions such as saving can partially undercut trade and insurance systems.

When savings is observed and controlled, the contract allows high-powered incentives, altering consumption and payoff streams so that the incentive and truth-telling constraints, discussed earlier in chapter 6, cause as little damage as possible. Doepke and Townsend (2006) show how to incorporate unobserved savings, in essence another set of incentive constraints, but the point remains that these are further restrictions on the design problem and cause a loss in welfare relative to full observability. These losses can be substantial. Observability can be recovered with tokens as immutable histories and rules for their use. In particular, one would not want to allow full convertibility of tokens to fiat, along the time line of implementation, as the information regained with those high-powered incentives would then be lost.[1] On the other hand, if this cannot be incorporated into the design, then that loss of welfare will result; but still, one can solve a more constrained design problem.

## 11.4 Lessons from Monetary Theory in Walrasian, Competitive Markets

A lesson from monetary theory is that fiat money can have value even if, intrinsically, it is worthless. The same arguments can apply to some cryptocurrencies. (Later in this chapter we return to distinguishing fiat from tokens.)

A key idea in monetary theory is that when strangers meet one another there can be an absence of double coincidence of wants. In a pairwise meeting, one party has something the other wants, which is half of the basis for a trade, but not the other way around. Money can serve as a medium of exchange in this instance; it serves as the other half of the trade, taken on by the party giving up something of intrinsic value, but only in order to be able to use it in the future, when the situation is reversed with another party.

Economic models try to simplify as much as possible to make this point and to be able to go on to consider regulation and policy. The first series of these models is outlined here and describes how intrinsically useless objects such as money can have value, whether paper currency and fiat money generally, or tokens and cryptocurrency. Again, the theory here does not yet make a distinction between the two—fiat versus token.

### 11.4.1 Models of Money with Endogenous Valuation

In Townsend (1980) an agent has fluctuating periodic endowments of a single good—for example with values 1,0,1,0—and that agent is paired at each date with someone on the opposite side of the sequence, 0,1,0,1 (see figure 11.1). But a given agent is never paired with the same person twice, hence capturing the idea that agents are meeting strangers. Related, there is no IOU as a promissory note to pay in the future, given the model construction of the separation in space and timing, that can come back to the issuer.

Endowments of the model should not be taken literally, but represent wage earnings for laborers and migrants, crop harvests for farmers, or profits for business, including trade as a

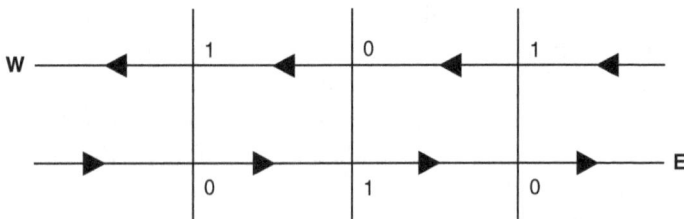

**Figure 11.1**
The Turnpike model of monetary exchange. The arrows denote the direction of travel. Each agent type starts at some trading post marked with a vertical line connecting the two lanes of the highway. The numbers denote the endowment of the consumption good of the agent as the agent travels. *Source:* Townsend (1980).

business as with a money transfer organization. Of note also in this model is that "endowments" average out to a constant, both other time for a given agent (though agents do discount the future, hence care about the timing) and also across agents at a point in time. Money is a balancing item, offsetting ups and downs for a given agent or across agents in the cross-section from those who are well endowed to those who are not. In a monetary equilibrium, worthless pieces of paper or tokens have value for buying goods; in the United States, this would be the US dollar (USD) price of consumption. Money is, in this sense, also a unit of account. Prices are in monetary terms. Finally, even in this simple model, money is being stored at any given moment by some agents over time from one period to the next, thus money is also a store of value. However, in a monetary equilibrium without any other intervention, with stable prices, there remain unexploited gains from trade, and consumption is moving with income even after monetary transactions (as discussed below). The optimal policy is to pay interest on currency so that inter-temporal marginal rates of substitution are equated.

In Woodford (1990), as in the model of Townsend (1980), public debt plays the role of providing liquidity. Such models are also used in Domeij and Ellingsen (2018).[2]

Borrowing and lending among agents in the above model do not necessarily complete the space of trades. As in Manuelli and Sargent (1988, 2010), there is a bond market for borrowers and lenders who meet for multiple periods sometimes, but not always and not forever; here itineraries are fixed but, more generally, one can consider segmented markets as the primitive. In addition, there are aggregate shocks. Given the timing of feasible trades, things do not balance out with debt alone. Money still plays a crucial role in smoothing the remaining residual fluctuations. The optimal monetary policy here, paying interest, has consequences for the distribution of income, which is different in the monetary equilibrium from the complete-markets, Walraisan equilibrium without money.

In a related model, the net incomes of households, producers, or traders are not deterministic, but rather are drawn as random variables. One might suppose realizations of income are drawn independently over time for a given agent and independently over agents at a point in time, as in Bewley (1983). Money is acquired when income is high via sales and spent to buy goods when income is low. Insurance contracts could have served the purpose of smoothing and, indeed, could do even better, especially if there is a large continuum of agents, so that the average state of the economy over agents at a point in time is constant. But in Bewley (1983), such contracts are ruled out *a priori* as simply not available, which can happen in reality when there is limited access to financial infrastructure (or lack of coordination). In this economic model, money is, if anything, an even more obvious store of value, a buffer stock that can be used against future shocks for self-insurance needs. An agent would always like to have some of it on hand, as income can always turn out to be low. Running out of money can be disastrous if incomes are near or at zero. So here again, money has value even if intrinsically useless. Also, as it stands, there is an irony: No finite amount of money is ever enough; it cannot replicate the full-insurance solution. Bewley (1983) makes a further point that interest on currency, though typically thought to be efficient, has a limit in this model. With too much interest a valued monetary equilibrium may not exist. Another contrast with the standard dictum: In the related model of Kehoe, Levine, and Woodford (1990), the stochastic variables are such that there should be inflation, not interest-yielding deflation.

Other models limit trade through the demographics of finite lives. Agents earn wage income when young, but at some point in the life cycle as they age they have zero labor earnings and need to rely on previous savings. Money can serve as social security, a bridge across the various generations, which was an insight of Samuelson (1958). Indeed, in this setting, stable money can achieve a full optimum. Adding more goods and variety in incomes, even within generations, allows more realism, as in Freeman (1996) and Green (1999). Money allows old debtors to repay old creditors from whom they previously borrowed and allows old creditors to buy a good $y$ from the young. Young debtors borrow to get good $x$. Here money is, even more obviously, a unit of account with a rationale in economic terms, as it is essential for trade. Given the environment, it must be on the other side of each commodity trade, in goods $x$ and $y$. If there are further obstacles to trade such as difficulty getting to market, then again there is scope for intervention (discussed below). That said, Tobin (1978) is skeptical that models such as overlapping generations are models of money.

It is enough in any of these models to keep track of who meets whom when and what is exchanged. This is all summarized in each model by a sequence of budget constraints, actions taken, and market-clearing conditions. Tokens, fiat or crypto, though intrinsically useless, have a social value in each model.

### 11.4.2 Testing for Inefficiency Using National Income Data

Arguments for social value beyond private value are not simply abstract. Monetary theory has empirical content and has been tested in actual economies. In particular, the literatures on overlapping generations and public debt (mentioned earlier) have been taken to macro data from national income accounts to judge whether economies are on efficient paths. If there is an overaccumulation of real capital, then the interest rate is lower than the natural rate of growth, which is clearly an inefficient outcome. Alternatively, if money has value as a valid bubble in equilibrium, less savings are put into productive assets and more are put into the bubble, raising the interest rate. Abel et al. (1989) propose a criterion for evaluating dynamic inefficiency that only involves comparisons of cash profits from capital, as a rate of return, with output coming from the history of the level of investment. They find that one cannot reject efficiency. Geerolf (2017) adjusts for land rent, taking it out, and adjusts the profits of entrepreneurs, a fraction of which is arguably simply opportunity-cost wages and not a real return. He finds some economies may have been on inefficient paths. One notes in the reported results that some Asian-miracle economies are among the excessive-investment economies. For them, the bubble is not big enough.

## 11.5 The Value of Money Comes from Cash in Advance or Payment of Taxes

Related and substantively important, the environments of the above and other monetary models can be generalized in a way that no equilibrium with valued money exists (Cass, Okuno, and Zilcha 1978; Green and Zhou 2005; Levine 1989).

But there are other ways to ensure that money has an economic value. Suppose money must be used in trade by fiat, or must be used to make certain required payments owed to the government. These arguments were given for fiat money but can also be applied to tokens. Utility tokens, for example, are necessary for the purchase of a good or service.

In an early paper in monetary economics, Starr (1974) specified, for tractability, a finite-horizon model. This raised the problem that in the last period, money could not have value because nobody would want it—there is no future with it. However, money in the Starr model had a value, nevertheless, because agents were required to pay taxes to the government with it at the end. Thus, money was always demanded in equilibrium, and the price could not fall to zero. Some see this as a realistic setting and one reason why fiat monies, as compared with tokens, have value in actual economies.

Likewise, the so-called cash-in-advance model of Clower (1967) specifies that fiat money is legal tender and thus must be acquired at least one period in advance in order to allow purchases with it in a given period. One could say that money has value in these models because of a legal stipulation requiring its use.[3] In the model of Lucas and Stokey (1983), some designated goods do not require cash in advance (the credit goods), but other goods do require cash in advance (the cash goods). Such models with credit goods allow real consumption loans and exchange in goods without money, but if there is at least a subset of crucial cash goods, however small, then the price of money cannot go to zero. Money must have a positive value in equilibrium.

## 11.6 A Hybrid Model of Positive Token Values

In summary, there are two ways of making money have value: endogenously in an equilibrium given the underlying environment, and exogenously by legal or other restrictions. Layering the two ways of modeling money delivers endogenous valuation of tokens in realistic economic settings. In this way, we can talk about innovations in payment systems using tokens which, nevertheless, take as given and utilize valued fiat money. It is not an "either/or" proposition. In contrast, much of the literature thinks of Bitcoin and other cryptocurrencies as competing with fiat money.

Specifically, one could start with an environment in which fiat money is endogenously valued in one of the equilibria or has to be used for some purpose, by fiat or taxes. Either way, fiat money then has value. In equilibrium, we can describe net earnings and profits of households, firms, and traders in fiat money terms, not as real commodities per se. Agents would be modeled as having indirect utility functions over money, or wealth more generally, conditioned on prevailing prices, rather than direct utility over commodities. Generously, this is one interpretation of Klein's (1976) demand for money.[4] With this outcome as a new starting point—a new underlying environment, as it were—there may be remaining gaps to be filled, as mentioned in the various models in the previous section on endogenous money. Thus, tokens could potentially help fill these gaps and can have endogenously determined positive value.

### 11.6.1 Implementation in Practice

With all of this, we now have set a more complicated but realistic stage for understanding the use of tokens in some distributed ledger systems.

We illustrate as an example the role of Velo tokens in the Lightnet system described earlier. To review, trades of MTOs are placed on the Stellar marketplace for exchange with token fiat monies. MTOs are traders in fiat monies and can be thought of as firms. They have their own fluctuating and time-varying profits, as do their potential customers, and hence would be looking for a mechanism of exchange that allows smoothing these fluctuations among them, within and across borders, so to speak, as if in one integrated economy. Indeed, some customers have a direct stake in what is going on in another country through migrants or business. The objects of trade among MTOs are not goods *per se* but these multiple fiat monies and these associated tokens, plus (if only indirectly) the Velo token. We come back to this idea momentarily. We turn first to a fundamental problem.

## 11.7 The Value of Money and Cryptocurrency: Social and Private Values Can Diverge

As is clear from the discussion above, valued money is a bubble in the sense that it can have social value and be priced despite being intrinsically useless. The fundamental welfare theorems of economics fail. Competitive equilibria without fiat money exist, but they are not typically optimal. Money is a social contrivance that allows bridges across generations, links among spatially separated agents, or buffers idiosyncratic shocks. But valued bubbles bring, in addition, the issues of indeterminate or unstable values, a multiplicity of equivalent monies, and hence unstable exchange rates and a multiplicity of equilibrium paths. Both of these points are lessons from monetary theory.

For example, Kareken and Wallace (1981) noted that without obstacles or fiat restrictions, the exchange rate between country-specific fiat monies is indeterminate. In the Samuelson (1958) model, as posited by Tirole (1985), for example, there are knife-edge good paths leading to optimal equilibria but many other paths leading to autarky with increasing inflation. Autarky itself is a valid equilibrium. If no one expects money to have value, it will not. More recently, Garratt and Wallace (2018) repeat these themes in a context featuring the coexistence of Bitcoin and fiat money. They also show how there can be a bubble in Bitcoin that can break at any moment with positive probability. Schilling and Uhlig (2018) also feature a version of the exchange-rate indeterminacy of the Kareken-Wallace (1981) model, but in a different model, similar to Townsend (1980), that is rationalized with spatial separation. They obtained as an additional "speculative" condition, implying that Bitcoin prices could form convergent supermartingales or submartingales.

### 11.7.1 How Can One Remove Indeterminacy of Token Values and Eliminate Bad Equilibria? The Lightnet System as an Example of Three Ways to Do It

The interest on Velo tokens can be generated by investing collateral fiat money in bonds that pay dividends in fiat currency. Likewise, one could view the Lightnet system as creating real capital for infrastructure with a positive rate of return, which in Fernández-Villaverde and Sanches (2016) creates scope for policy to achieve an optimal allocation. As Garratt and Wallace (2018) put it, indeterminacy in the value of a money is removed in all models if real dividends on money are paid. Lightnet does pay interest on lockup accounts. These have the potential to pin down the coin to a fiat money exchange rate just as in the monetary model. Ideally promised-to-pay interest would be in fiat, though airdrops in tokens that pay comparable rates of return given exchange rate of tokens to fiat could come close if the commitment is maintained. This can be programmed in as smart contracts.

A second device is to impose some required demand. The Velo token is used as collateral backing trades in fiat monies, so it is required for trade similar to the way money is required for purchases in cash-in-advance models. The value of transfer in fiat is required to be commensurate with the value of Velo tokens. Of course, the contingent aspect of collateral is programmed in as a smart contract.

Likewise, some cryptocurrencies such as Ethereum require tokens to pay for the "gas"—that is, to pay costs—to do contract validation. In this sense they are utility coins. Of course, this imposes some distortions that in the ideal equilibrium would not be needed. But still indeterminacy can be a big problem, so there seems to be a trade-off that needs to be explored.

A third device is backing, which Lightnet has not adopted explicitly, but this is an important subject in its own right.

## 11.8 Stable Coins

A stable coin is a cryptocurrency tied to the value of an underlying asset. Such coins are intended to solve the volatility problem where the price of cryptocurrencies traded on exchanges has been erratic. There are various types of stable coins.

The following descriptions draw on a report by Blockdata .tech (2018). One type is asset-backed off-chain. These are stable coins backed by a "regular" fiat currency such as USD or euro, precious metals, or other real-world assets. Some require trust in an opaque and centralized third party to hold deposits or collateral. Among others, Tether stands out, supposedly entirely backed by US dollars, but evidently that was not the case.[5] It appears some of the reserves arguably intended for redemption were lent to another company, Bitfinex.

The stable coin Libra to be issued under the Facebook consortium will be backed by a reserve fund. The details may be evolving, as Libra is not yet operational. According to one source, the day-to-day value of Libra is to be pegged to the average value of a basket of world currencies made up of US dollars, UK pounds, euros, and Swiss francs (Roberts 2019). According to another source, the backing is a basket of bank deposits and short-term government securities, in which case Libra is more like an exchange-traded fund than a fiat-backed stable coin (Acheson 2019).

A second type of stable coin, asset-backed on-chain, as in Klein (1976), is backed by cryptocurrencies. An example is backing by Ethereum's Ether. In this case the stability of the cryptocurrency backing may be in doubt as, again, many cryptocurrencies fluctuate in value, which is the problem motivating stable coins from the get-go. MakerDAO stands out as a salient example, issuing a stable coin Dai against Ether deposits.

Interestingly, the backing mechanism is a relatively sophisticated smart contract (Makerdao.com 2017, 2019). Following the MakerDAO discussion closely, collateralized debt positions (CDPs) hold collateral assets deposited by a user and in return for new Dai, but as a debt contract. The debt effectively locks the deposited collateral assets, Ether, inside the CDP until it is later covered by paying back an equivalent amount of Dai relative to Ether at then-contemporary value. At this point the owner can withdraw his collateral and that Dai is extinguished. This is akin to a repo transaction. As with repo, active CDPs are always collateralized in excess, meaning that the market value of the collateral is (much) higher than the value of the debt. Accordingly,

> When the value of collateral increases, borrowers are able to create new dai (up to the safe ratio). When the USD value of collateral falls, borrowers can choose to either repay borrowed dai or deposit more collateral, as their position approaches the liquidation ratio. Borrowers who allow their positions to fall below the imposed safe ratio risk forced liquidation. Forced liquidation is Makers way of ensuring that the amount of collateral backing circulating dai remains within safe parameters. (Makerdao.com 2019)

A third type of stable coin as described in Blockdata.tech (2018) is a Seigniorage-style algorithm: "Smart contracts" automatically expand and contract the supply of noncollateralized currency using algorithms to maintain value. If the value of a stable coin drops below its par value, the algorithm buys the coin (with accumulated profits), decreasing supply with the goal of raising the price. But if the price remains below par and such profits are exhausted, then the algorithm issues a bond, a promise to pay in the future from future profits, and uses the proceeds to buy the coin. Investors (lenders) believing in a self-fulfilling prophesy count on future stable value at par (or higher).

Between fully backed and algorithmic types are stable coins that pay variable interest as a function of reserves. At one extreme the interest rate is meant to attract buyers, as in interest arbitrage across multicountry fiat currencies (which has not worked well). On the other extreme are fully backed coins where the interest on securities or appreciation of currencies accrues to the holder of the coin. The experience of maintaining fiat money exchange rates via interest rate policies has been mixed, with exchange rates violating covered and uncovered interest arbitrage.

Another nontrivial caveat: Price-fixing schemes are doomed to failure (Townsend 1977). Even if the relative price of two distinct objects is set at the average expected price, random walks ensure that any bound will be surpassed with probability one; no amount of reserves is ever enough. The price must change.

## 11.9 The Need for Commitment in Cryptocurrency Design

Monetary policy can be time inconsistent if there is no commitment. Lucas and Stokey (1983) make this point in a model where money has value due to a cash-in-advance constraint. Essentially, the government is always tempted to tax money balances once they are there, via inflation. Subsequent literature has tried to alleviate this by management of real and nominal assets and the maturity structure of debt. The conditionality and preprogrammed nature of distributed ledger protocols is a direct advantage in this context. Xandri (2016) makes this point, how a central bank can acquire a good reputation, and Fernández-Villaverde and Sanches (2016) hint at this in their frequent references to automata, immutability, and quasi commitment. Credible commitments can be loaded in up front as part of the algorithmic design of the digital reserve bank as smart contracts entered on ledgers. Central banks can change rules, though in practice in the countries within the OECD, central banks handle time-inconsistency issues well. That said, political authorities try to push them off it.

## 11.10 Interest Rate Policy for the Digital Reserve Bank: Insights from the Monetary Models

Social systems designed to achieve optimal allocation can require interventionist, activist liquidity policy. This becomes clear through the lens of the models of money enumerated at the outset. These lessons then apply to the token management of the digital reserve system.

Spatial separation is a key friction, realistic in many settings, which gives rise to limited trade, as noted in Townsend (1980). Because of timing and frictions, agents in equilibrium with valued money will periodically run out of previously accumulated cash. That is, there are binding constraints. Agents are optimizing, but marginal rates of inter-temporal substitution are not equated over agents. To achieve a full Pareto optimum, a situation in which no one can be made better off without making someone else worse off, marginal rates of substitution must be equated to each other and to the natural discount rate, as noted earlier. For this candidate for a new equilibrium to be valid, those holding tokens must find that tokens effectively bear interest at a rate that is the same natural rate of preference discount. Tokens are still valued in the spatial models, but the obstacle to trade, the cost of carrying tokens, is removed.

If the effective interest rate, the real return, is achieved via deflation of tokens, then the real balance value of tokens is increasing. Either way, as interest or deflation, some tokens must be taxed out of the system. This tax in the model is an imposed lump sum and applies only when agents hold positive token balances. In the model this is known in advance. In practice, it will be crucial to find taxes that do not influence behavior on the margin. Interest should be paid and taxes implemented, whether in fiat or in tokens. Likewise, interest on tokens encourages users to hold more of them, rather than assets that otherwise dominate, related to the indeterminacy discussion earlier. Fees on transactions that reflect true costs of transactions, in technology or risk, should be implemented. This works toward equating marginal costs with marginal benefits.

A related example of an active policy comes from historical experience. The Federal Reserve Bank in the United States was created initially neither for full employment nor for price stability, but rather to provide an elastic currency (Sprague 1910). There were heavy seasonal movements in the demand for currency. For example, currency was needed to buy grain from farmers at harvest, to move the crop. But bank liabilities were backed by gold, so withdrawals of deposits from banks to pay farmers put stress on the system. Banks in agricultural regions could not create their own money-like objects. Instead, they had to find value by calling in loans from their correspondent banks in New York. In turn, city banks that had funded margin accounts on the New York stock market called in these loans and this led, according to conventional wisdom, to financial crises.

In the corresponding analog models of Freeman (1996) and Green (1999), creditors and debtors do not necessarily meet at the "right" time. A fraction of debtors arrives late, and a fraction of creditors leaves early. This naturally complicates the debt settlement process and leads to inefficiencies and fluctuations in interest rates. It is resolved by having a central bank, or the digital reserve bank, engage in open-market operations or in security transactions with the securitized notes that the bank issues (based on segregated collateral of correspondents) to control the requisite means of payment and smooth the interest rate.[6]

In another version of these models (Chandrasekhar, Townsend, and Xandri 2018), individual-level market participation is determined as if by an exogenous random shock. Entities with high value are those that are in the borrowing/lending market when the market is thin, when risk aversion is high, when risk from variable returns is high, and when the remaining players are judged to be important (high Pareto weight). Reserve bank liquidity should be directed ex ante to these key players.

For each of these examples of policy, microdata are needed on transactions. Wallace (2014) argues, for example, that one can know optimal policy ought to be active, not laissez-faire, but not know without more information which way it goes: inflation or deflation. With the digital reserve bank as a notary as in Lightnet, for example, data would be available. In principle, this could be organized by financial accounts, tying back into an earlier discussion in chapter 3.

# 12
# Summary and Conclusion

Distributed ledgers have the potential to transform economic organization and financial structure, yet the subject is embroiled in controversy, hype, and lack of consistent terminology, as chapter 1 makes clear. Rather than get hung up on proper definitions about what a distributed ledger is and isn't, and how broadly or narrowly the term should be interpreted, we focus instead on the economics of what distributed ledgers can do by breaking down the concepts and analyzing the key individual components. We also compare and contrast the economic framework with the frameworks of the computer science and data management disciplines, clarifying the terminology and the technology where possible. Finally, we attempt to combine economics and computer science and forge new ground.

One of the ingredients missing from much of the discussion of distributed ledgers is the context and clarity in the application to actual economies. Chapter 2 thus begins with conceptual background on what economists mean by an economy, natural welfare functions to judge efficiency, and ideal systems of measurement. Many of these ingredients come together in the Townsend Thai project, which is featured frequently in examples in subsequent chapters, but this book is about much more than that.

Chapters 3 through 6 describe distributed ledgers in terms of the key, though familiar, component parts: ledgers as accounts, e-messages and e-transfers of value, cryptography, and contracts, including multiparty mechanisms. We put each in context and provide examples, emphasizing what each of these parts of digital ledger technology brings to the table, one at a time.

For the first component, ledgers, in chapter 3 we link the ledgers of cryptocurrencies to a statement of currency flow as a standard financial account and to currency as a balance-sheet item. Cash flow accounts in Thai villages are presented as an example; in this context currency flows are reasonably well measured and have been used in analysis, but of course, the idea is much more general. Financial accounts are a universal concept. The ledgers of DLT are then put into this context, taking an additional step which, in essence, is simply creating a common integrated database of cash flows across households and the associated balance-sheet entries. With this, one uncovers discrepancies, not unlike how the use of DLT can help in the reconciliation of trades. A related analogy: Standard financial accounts were an invention associated with double-entry bookkeeping, for more accurate measurement, a huge innovation at the time. Likewise, DLT enhances measurement across diverse parties.

Relatedly, the DLT ledgers could be used with transaction data to create standard financial accounts—namely, the income statement in addition to a complete balance sheet and complete statement of cash flow. These accounts are useful in analysis, and for policy, as illustrated by two timely examples: the impact of tariffs and regional isolation and drawing a distinction among various sources of liquidity, not simply cash. Likewise, forging a connection between DLT and financial accounts makes clear the even greater potential for DLT, though not yet realized—what we might term *consensus categorization*.

Chapter 3 concludes with a revealing summary of issues known from the science of database management. There are key impossibility theorems for decentralized systems: One cannot have all of consistency, accuracy, and partitioning. Yet systems that are periodically synchronized, and thus consistent, require costly communication and do not scale up, as at some point in the process of validation every node is connected to every other. This conundrum is sometimes not stated baldly or faced squarely. Trusted third parties do solve this problem, hence their appeal, but this centralization not only requires trust but raises the issue of data integrity and data security cyber-risk issues. One conclusion of this chapter is that hybrid systems with partial meshes, in which not all nodes connect to each other, may be best for many applications. An illustrative example is Lightning Network, which shifts small transactions to a cryptographically secure "off-chain" environment so that only large netting transactions need to be directly settled on the blockchain. Thus, although hybrid systems between the end points of strictly hierarchical database systems do emerge in practice (ignoring incentives and fully connected network meshes, which exacerbate privacy concerns), they are not necessarily a deliberate choice among the universe of possibilities. The economics literature provides clear examples of how costly connections among agents can lead to constrained-optimal partitioning (numbers in a cluster and how many clusters). A second conclusion of this chapter is that more work needs to be done on optimal design.

For the second component of DLT, e-transfers and e-messages, we compare and contrast in chapter 4 two countries, Thailand and Sweden, from high to low ratios of currency to GDP, respectively. For Thailand, there are large welfare losses to the current reliance on paper currency. For Sweden one worry, ironically, is the other way, at least in the near term—groups vulnerable to the disappearance of currency. We then feature an innovation, e-money, for a country in between, Kenya, where M-Pesa has generated large welfare gains. This is done with a trusted third party, Safaricom, and without cryptocurrency, though the ledgers of Safaricom resemble tokens in some ways. The key is allowing easy ins and outs from Kenyan shillings to cell credits, facilitating transfers from urban migrants back to villages, for better risk-sharing and poverty reduction.

Some caveats bring us back to the featured issues of this book. For one, in the Kenyan context with Safaricom, trust is less obvious than it might seem when taking into account the larger financial system, with banks indirectly holding accounts, the Kenyan shillings that were turned in for e-tokens. For another, a relatively undeveloped part of value exchange is the infrastructure for liquidity, a common shortcoming in Kenya with its dual currency system and in New York financial markets in securities and central bank reserves. Ironically, most exchanges for DLT cryptocurrency that provide liquidity in and out of fiat monies and other cryptocurrencies rely on traditional technology with trusted third parties and not on DLT. That is, the tokens that feature absence of third-party trust rely on such trust for market exchange. The exchanges that are DLT-based are currently slow and illiquid. This highlights an area where further work is needed. However, we will not fall into the trap of insisting that all parts of a system be decentralized, as some do. That is, money needs to be decentralized, hence cryptocurrency, or exchanges need to be decentralized, hence digital assets. To the contrary, hybrids may well be desirable but, again, what is striking is the surprising lack of work in this area of overall optimal design of institutions and markets for a given economy.

E-transfers naturally raise issues related to cryptography and verification of messages if there is not universal trust in a single third party. As covered in chapter 5, ideas for overcoming lack of trust in parts of a financial system are ancient, dating back to Mesopotamia, where sealed clay envelopes containing tokens were used as a manifest of shipments from supplier to destination to guard against tampering in between. Similarly, in medieval times, tally sticks split into pieces were used, with the stock circulating as money that uniquely matched the foil held by the borrower, checked on redemption. More recently, but before Bitcoin, we have secure multiparty communication, IBM crypto express cards, public vs. private keys, and zero-knowledge proofs and protocols. The chapter on cryptography contains an important discussion of the various validation systems used, from Bitcoin's proof of work, to proof of stake, to federated decentralized systems of trust, which require a listing of trusted nodes, but a list that is different across different nodes. To some, the term *distributed ledger* refers uniquely to only some but not all of these decentralized validation systems, though that point of view seems excessively narrow. More generally, but still narrow in the view of this book, the consensus part of DLT is often taken as a defining characteristic. But one can easily lose sight of the underlying economic purpose of a system, and why messages need to be validated in the first place, if at all, other than to claim the title of being decentralized.

This brings us to mechanism design in chapter 6 and the fourth economic component of distributed ledgers. For contracts, we highlight from standard contract literature the needed distinctions to get at the meaning of the word *trust* as in "trusted third parties," as featured in the introduction. These distinctions include full commitment versus limited commitment; contract theory allows the latter, but this does not preclude some trades. Likewise, from contract theory and mechanism design we can speak of incentive compatibility for actions and truth-telling for messages for initial and interim unobserved states. Lack of trust in this specific sense is crucial in the design but is not an insuperable barrier. Related, it is key to prevent parties from pulling out or not performing. Default has remedies in collateral and/or reputation made explicit under long-term contracting. Reneging and a restriction to time consistency can be remedied with commitment. Problems of collusion and nonuniqueness in implementation have remedies in better design. We need to get specific across the various trust aspects, and contract theory helps us do that, especially in hybrid systems.

For the contract part of DLT innovation, we feature the key technical capabilities of smart contracts, highlighting the commitment in entering into the agreement and carrying it out, the immutability of its terms, and the conditionality aspects that help resolve the various trust problems, as agreed-to options are executed automatically as a function of the state. Smart contracts help to mitigate underlying frictions in the environment. Key concepts here also include states of the system and transitions, commands, validity consensus, unique consensus, notaries and nonunique consensus, multiple trusting or nontrusted notaries, public and private nodes, oracles, and broadcast communication versus selectively private communication.

A key point is that the various aspects of trust and incentives that come from mechanism design can be implemented on smart contracts and hence have implications for the messages, transfers, and recommendations that would be happening in real time. If messages and so on satisfy underlying incentive and truth-telling constraints, then the only reason to validate messages is because of faulty but not malicious nodes. This seems like a key distinction, but it is rarely made. Furthermore, depending on the contract, messages need not be sent of a domain of states, as in costly state verification, and past histories can be summarized by key statistics as in the use of promised utility and utility threats to collapse the dimensional of the problem.

Economists have had these mechanisms in mind, and so in some sense have taken smart contracts for granted without realizing it. However, DLT and smart-contract technology are more limited than it might appear at first blush, raising conceptual issues. The "planner" problem of mechanism design is a metaphor for economists, not taken literally *per se*, but in the context here is it clear that one must specify how contracts and multiparty agreements are entered into and validated and how they are executed over time. The doorkeepers and notaries involved with smart-contract execution, if single entities, are hierarchical features, though competing, nontrusting notaries conjure up the image of more decentralized systems. Decentralizing on Ethereum can be quite costly, suggesting that the writing of code, validation, and numerical computation be done offline. On the positive side, some of the underlying basics of mechanism design survive some substantial limitations, though the definition and nature of an optimal arrangement would change. A version of the revelation principle works with noisy messages, and with no communication at all, so one need not abandon mechanism design when facing the reality of imperfect messaging. Though there are impossibility results regarding consensus in the economics literature, there are also contributions on the effectiveness of multiple repeat messages and how iterations of decentralized validation can be truncated and achieve coordination. It seems some of these are not yet incorporated into consensus protocols.

Chapter 7 continues the discussion of "decentralization," highlighting some paradoxical results in mechanism design. Ledgers can be partitioned by the information that agents in a multiparty smart contract are supposed to have or, better put, not have. Here the contract node plays a crucial preprogrammed role, receiving all incentive-compatible communication but not necessarily broadcasting all incoming messages. Explicit randomization can be done at the level of the contract node as planner, to ensure a gain from concealment and keeping secrets. Another instance: the delegation to a preprogrammed, third-party custodian to deal with private and public shocks that allow back- and front-loading in contracts. That function looks quite centralized. A final section of chapter 7 looks at portable physical tokens, privately held but voluntarily disclosed, as a decentralized way of recording key aspects of history, also implementable with partitioned ledgers. Multiple colored tokens can also have a role, though, again, in some environments we do not want to display full history. This part of the mechanism design literature is of course about design and does not appear to be incorporated into the computer science discussion of validation.

Chapters 8 and 9 go on to feature an example where innovation would allow large gains. As noted in chapter 8, in Thailand and across other countries in Southeast Asia, traditional formal financial infrastructure is currently extremely limited. From Asian Development Bank studies, we know there are large gaps in services for credit, saving, payments, and insurance. From the Townsend Thai project we know that informal risk-sharing is good for idiosyncratic risk. There are in effect village money markets replete with credit chains that resemble the sophistication of advanced country systems. But there are shortfalls in reallocating risk across villages and regions, and management of cash is inefficient in rural areas. Interventions can make a difference. A government village fund program had positive impacts on consumption, borrowing, investment, profits, and intermediation. Yet this was uneven. Those without kin did not benefit nearly as much, and villages remain largely disconnected from one another. The ironic virtue of DLT work in Thailand is that it is easier to start from scratch in implementing optimal designs, as gains are large and there are no coordination or consortia problems.

Innovations in this Southeast Asia context can come in two related forms. First, individual smart contracts are given as examples of how to take advantage of distributed ledger capability: escrow with nonbanks; savings products for automated deposit and portfolio management; and securitized waterfall payments along the path of supply chains from buyer to seller to employee loans. A second form is contract competition with open access to providers and free entry, as in general equilibrium models with an intermediary broker sector. Here then we are combining the needed micro side (the contracts) with the more macro side (general equilibrium), incentives of participants in open markets, and whether or not this will work, drawing on theory literature.

Featured as an example of innovation is EvryNet, an intelligent financial automation operating system that aims to provide open-source banking services and financial contracts to unbanked and underbanked populations. An interoperable smart-contract platform enables not only traditional banks but also microfinance institutions and others to initiate and execute banking products and financial contracts. Contracts can be provided at competitive prices for computer memory (storage) and computation power. A rating system tracks the performances of providers.

Chapter 9 features two payment systems on distributed ledgers. One, an experiment, is Project Jasper from the Bank of Canada, which is designed for domestic interbank payment settlement and is focused on payments. The role of the notary node is played by the Bank of Canada. Phase 2 of Project Jasper appears to be one of the first instances of a central queue within a DLT platform for payments, for matching and netting. A matching algorithm on a distributed ledger platform employs the language of states and conditionality. Netting promotes funding efficiency and smoother intraday payments flow. In Project Jasper, parties see only their own activity, a traditional point of view, while the role of the unique notary is played by the Bank of Canada. It is a sophisticated multiparty platform taking advantage of smart contract possibilities.

The second featured payment system is Lightnet, creating for money transfer operators (MTOs) in Southeast Asia a highly liquid, decentralized settlement layer on a permissioned blockchain. Remittances in fiat money in Southeast Asia have transfer fees currently at 7.1%. The high transfer fees are partly the result of legacy technology in the formal sector and limited access to formal currency exchange markets. The Velo network is a settlement layer that avoids direct transfers of fiat money yet enables participants to conduct cross-border transactions efficiently. An optimized liquidity-management layer will efficiently search for offsetting cross-country balances to allow for expedient clearing while minimizing risk. MTOs can be viewed as agents with varying underlying balance sheets hit by their customers' needs for trade and hence credit and insurance. Some MTOs are already engaged in a contractual bilateral relationship, with both of their fiat credit lines supporting their financial obligations bound by a bilateral agreement. The point is that Lightnet can allow the implementation of constrained-optimal contract arrangements implemented on distributed ledgers, as envisioned in the examples on credit and insurance described earlier. That should not appear as abstract and otherworldly, as it has its real-world counterpart here. Notably, economic outcomes under contracts, data acquired, and data disseminated are all endogenous and codetermined.

Chapter 10 addresses some regulatory issues or, better put, some regulatory opportunities. Distributed ledgers mitigate, if not eliminate, bank and market runs through time-stamped and immutable records of the histories of transactions. For that last result on runs, caveats from computer science come into play—namely, latency on networks—but potential remedies are noted.

The limits of contract competition are noted here, too. Competition among providers can fail to complete the financial system because of unexploited complementarities and lack of coordination in a Nash equilibrium, even in environments in which all players are tiny such that no player has any mass. But there is a message in this for regulators. Traditional categories, separating insurance from credit, for example, may block necessary innovation. Relatedly, a key issue for regulation is the time line of competition and when to impose exclusivity; for example, free competition ex ante could be fine, but with exclusivity and restrictions on trade ex post. Regulators should not come to this subject with the point of view that "anything goes" or that everything is bad.

Other model environments make clear that consensus and public ledgers can be needed for coordination and prudential regulation. A theorem in economics on the impossibility of decentralized monetary exchange is quite relevant. Knowledge of identities of agents, histories of trade and payments, and initial excess demands are needed for implementation of optimal allocations, not simply pairwise knowledge of those contemporaneously matched but also from others with whom the contemporaneous set of matched traders, the payment parties, have not been matched previously. Put simply, the history of trades needs to appear on the common immutable ledger. Implementation of a Walrasian optimum in a decentralized way is both forward- and backward-looking. One has to know where the system should be headed, and the remaining options in the future to get there, hence what trades have been accomplished in the past and what trades are needed now in order to make this feasible.

For another example, circulating private debt is the medium of exchange for contemporaneous transactions in both short-term noncirculating securities and consumption commodities. Yet there can be many equilibria that achieve the Pareto optimal target; for example, either all the debts that are allowed to circulate could be issued by initial parties in one of the two locations or by the parties in the other, second location. But by assumption, in the example environment of the informationally decentralized model, there is no way for traders in one location to know what is going on in the other. Mismatch is likely, with too much or too little debt issued, with resulting crashes later. These conflicts and the need for coordination are likely to arise with multiple cryptocurrencies.

Chapter 11 addresses head-on issues surrounding cryptocurrency and tokens. The subject inevitably brings controversy, as advocates and detractors of Bitcoin argue about whether or not cryptocurrencies are monies and whether they should or should not be allowed to be alternatives to fiat monies. It is here in particular that monetary theory and mechanism design can be brought to the table, though typically this is not the case. First, as a reminder to the reader, chapter 11 reviews the various objects, including private objects that are considered money even under standard definitions, though the best measures look at velocity and frequency of use in exchange. Typically, there are multiple media of exchange in use in a given economy, so from that standpoint it is a bit surprising that detractors do not see room for more. Nevertheless, the idea persists that there is room for fiat money only and not cryptocurrency. To the contrary, tokens can be a useful tool in the implementation of mechanism design problems, and there one does not want fungibility between the two. From monetary theory we know that models with endogenously valued money can have good equilibria, Pareto improving on autarky, even though money is an intrinsically useful object—a sharp reminder to central bankers who make this charge against cryptocurrency as if to say crypto values have to be zero and the rest is speculation. Actually, some bubbles can be good, and there is a companion empirical literature. Nevertheless, both equilibria with value money and equilibria with valued tokens can suffer from indeterminacy and many other potential equilibria, not as extreme as autarky but with inflation and the value of fiat money, or cryptocurrency, going to zero or with fluctuations, the latter a potential explanation for what we are observing for cryptocurrency exchange rates. A way to ensure fiat money has value, with a positive lower bound, is to require its use in the payment of taxes or require its use in exchange by fiat. There are many models that follow those lines for modeling fiat. However, the same argument applies to cryptocurrencies that are utility tokens, required as part of business operations with smart contracts, even if at the same time these tokens are traded on exchanges. Finally, fiat and crypto monies can coexist and play useful roles, if the use of one only—say, fiat—would leave economic gaps and room for the other. One type of stable coin achieves value by backing, similar to the concept of narrow banks with 100% reserves. The discussion of other stable coins seems to suffer from limited knowledge of the monetary-theory literature or lessons from fiat exchange rates managed by central banks. An algorithmic digital reserve system with smart contracts on distributed ledgers can offer not only commitment, it could implement optimal activist token policies suggested by the monetary models, armed with transactions data from the distributed ledger.

# Notes

**Chapter 1**

1. See also Mills et al. (2016).

2. Illustrative examples are featured on the IBM Blockchain website. See "Hyperledger Fabric" (https://www.ibm.com/blockchain/hyperledger) and https://mediacenter.ibm.com/media/1_9bo2zfip?mhsrc=ibmsearch_a&mhq=maersk.

3. Chiu and Koeppl (2017) document that more than 740 cryptocurrencies have been introduced as of July 2016.

4. For a stark example of the trade-off between smart contracts on public ledgers and the industry collusion this allows, see Cong and He (2019).

5. According to the Bank for International Settlements (BIS 2018, 91), "Decentralised technology of cryptocurrencies, however sophisticated, is a poor substitute for the solid institutional backing of money." In other words, the cryptocurrencies require independent and accountable central banks. Shin (2018) makes this case based on the economics of user fees for Bitcoin. The fees are high because of deliberately engineered congestion, but that, in turn, limits the use of cryptocurrency as money. Denison, Lee, and Martin (2016) also draw their conclusion: Trustless, expensive decentralized systems such as Bitcoin are not needed, they argue.

6. A related, though opposite, example of slow-moving innovations is a preexisting invention that waits until there is a shock and then the system jumps to a new configuration; see Crouzet, Gupta, and Mezzanotti (2019).

7. Relatedly, the public sector is not limited to reacting to potential and actual private-sector innovations, sometimes with the purpose of preventing them, as with fintechs in some countries, not to mention Bitcoin. The public sector can also take a leading role, as stated in the BIS committee report. An example featuring the Canadian central bank is detailed later in this book. Sweden naturally features its public and private partnerships (PPPs). Sweden's past and present modernization of its payment system provides many salient examples of public innovation—for example, the first issue of paper currency, the highest contemporary user of e-transfers, the recently implemented fast payments system, Swish, and perhaps in the future the first with e-coins (Ingves 2016).

**Chapter 3**

1. We do not have a natural beginning point, unlike the genesis state in cryptography for the first e-coins, hence we need the measurement of a baseline.

2. For a discussion, see Kestenbaum (2012).

3. See also Bersem, Perotti, and von Thadden (2013) for a related discussion of welfare comparisons.

**Chapter 4**

1. Ironically, the Swedish Post and Telecom Authority (2017) reports that currency infrastructure is being depleted. Cash is becoming less accessible. Many banks have stopped managing cash with ATMs, which are disappearing. In a growing number of stores around the country, it is not possible to pay with cash today. There is a common worry that people who use only currency may become isolated outside the payment system unless they find the support and help they need. See also Erlandsson and Guibourg (2018). The Riksbank is concerned that without currency, all payment devices in the country are provided by the private sector, which is one reason it is considering a central bank digital currency.

2. See Jack, Suri, and Townsend (2010) for this discussion.

3. See Carlson (2017) for a study of one of them, and more recently Bharadwaj, Jack and Suri (2018).

4. See also Lagos and Wright (2005).

## Chapter 5

1. "Those tally sticks met an unfortunate end. The system was finally abolished and replaced by paper ledgers in 1834. To celebrate, it was decided to burn the sticks—six centuries of irreplaceable monetary records—in a coal-fired stove in the House of Lords, rather than letting parliamentary staff take them home for firewood. Burning a cartload or two of tally sticks in a coal-fired stove is a wonderful way to start a raging chimney fire. So it was that the House of Lords, then the House of Commons, and almost the entire Palace of Westminster—a building as old as the tally stick system itself—was burned to the ground" (Harford 2017).

2. This definition comes from Neha Narula in personal correspondence with the author in January 2019.

3. This material is drawn from Ray (2018), Lumenauts.com (2018), and u/PumpkinFeet (2018).

4. See, for example, Athey et al. (2016); Casey et al. (2018); Foley, Karlsen, and Putnins (2019); Griffin and Shams (2018); Prat and Walter (2018); Cong, He, and Li (2018); Cao, Cong, and Yang (2018); Janin, Gervais, and Mamageishvili (2019).

5. See also Dandekar et al. (2012).

## Chapter 6

1. See also Green and Oh (1991) and Karaivanov and Townsend (2014).

2. For examples of this second piece, see Abreu, Pearce, and Stacchetti (1990), Green (1987), Phelan and Townsend (1991), and Spear and Srivastava (1987).

3. See Ligon, Thomas, and Worrall (2002) for penalties.

4. See Phelan and Townsend (1991) for an example of how to impose this constraint and what difference it makes for the optimal contract design.

5. See section 10 in Harris and Townsend (1981), and for examples of an implementation literature, see Moore and Repullo (1990) and Palfrey and Srivastava (1989).

6. But see Hart and Moore (2007) for a discussion of incomplete contracts.

7. For a compelling video of how technologies like these can work in practice, see Inveniam Capital Partners (2019) for the context of real-estate transactions.

## Chapter 7

1. China has implemented regulation to prevent this kind of delegation to platforms—namely, that platforms be pass-through only. The Chinese government's decision was motivated by incidents of outright fraud.

2. For a generalized treatment of communication in games over time, see Myerson (1986).

3. One clarification, the idea of coloring coins came about as a way to overcome initial limitations in Bitcoin. With the current version of Ethereum, this is no longer needed, but the point about distinguishing histories remains.

## Chapter 9

1. Reconciliation and reliable registries were mentioned in the introduction to this book.

2. See Güntzer, Jungnickel, and Leclerc (1998) and Kuussaari (1996) for further discussion of algorithms for clearing and risks.

3. See Monnet and Nellen (2014) for theoretical modeling of central counterparty (CCP) clearing. Also related, see Monetary Authority of Singapore and the Association of Banks in Singapore (2017, 6) on running its own innovation center: "The prototypes successfully demonstrate several points. Firstly, that key functions of a RTGS [real-time gross settlement] system such as fund transfer, queueing mechanism and gridlock resolution can be achieved through different techniques and solution designs. Secondly, decentralizing the key functions of a RTGS system may not only mitigate the inherent risks of a centralized system, such as single point of failure, but may also affirm the promised benefits of DLT, for example cryptographic security and immutability."

4. One vision for Velo has the token as a utility at a fixed price. If there are markets for Velo exchanges against fiat, new issues are raised, and addressed, in chapter 11 on cryptocurrency.

## Chapter 10
1. See Townsend (1980), for example, for a more general discussion of why money holding is a distortion and money should bear interest.

## Chapter 11
1. Agents may be tempted to make deals on the side, a threat that could reduce multiple currencies to one. However, for there to be an effect, agents would have to hand over their private keys to a third party, and unless this is all in the same family, this type of off-path deviation could be anticipated to be minimal.

2. See also Angeletos, Collard, and Dellas (2016) and Diamond (1965).

3. See also Bryant and Wallace (1984).

4. An exception, Klein (1976), talks of a money to which other monies are tied. Indeed, we can introduce the idea of having multiple-country fiat monies, with value by fiat for example, and think of the dollar standard across currencies.

5. For more on the Tether stable coin, see Morris (2019) and De (2019).

6. For more information, see also Townsend (1989).

# References

Abel, Andrew B., N. Gregory Mankiw, Lawrence H. Summers, and Richard J. Zeckhauser. 1989. "Assessing Dynamic Efficiency: Theory and Evidence." *Review of Economic Studies* 56 (1): 1–19.

Abreu, Dilip, David Pearce, and Ennio Stacchetti. 1990. "Toward a Theory of Discounted Repeated Games with Imperfect Monitoring." *Econometrica* 58 (5): 1041–1063.

Acemoglu, Daron, and Fabrizio Zilibotti. 1997. "Was Prometheus Unbound by Chance? Risk, Diversification, and Growth." *Journal of Political Economy* 105 (4): 709–751.

Acheson, Noelle. 2019. "Libra Isn't a Cryptocurrency. It's a Glimpse of a New Asset Class." *Coindesk*, July 7. https://www.coindesk.com/libra-isnt-a-cryptocurrency-its-a-glimpse-of-a-new-asset-class.

Adrian, Tobias, and Hyun Song Shin. 2009. "Money, Liquidity, and Monetary Policy." Federal Reserve Bank of New York Staff Report No. 360.

Aiyagari, S. Rao. 1994. "Uninsured Idiosyncratic Risk and Aggregate Saving." *Quarterly Journal of Economics* 109 (3): 659–684.

Alvarez, Fernando, and Francesco Lippi. 2009. "Financial Innovation and the Transactions Demand for Cash." *Econometrica* 77 (2): 363–402.

Alvarez, Fernando, Anan Pawasutipaisit, and Robert M. Townsend. 2018. "Cash Management in Village Thailand: Positive and Normative Implications." MIT Working Paper.

Amberg, Niklas, Tor Jacobson, Erik von Schedvin, and Robert M. Townsend. 2016. "Curbing Shocks to Corporate Liquidity: The Role of Trade Credit." National Bureau of Economic Research (NBER) Working Paper No. 22286.

Angeletos, George-Marios, Fabrice Collard, and Harris Dellas. 2016. "Public Debt as Private Liquidity: Optimal Policy." NBER Working Paper No. 22794.

Aronoff, Daniel J. 2019. "On the Resilience of the Blockchain to Double-Spend Attacks." MIT Working Paper.

ASEAN. 2017. "ASEAN Statistical Leaflet—Selected Key Indicators 2017." ASEAN Secretariat, Jakarta. https://www.aseanstats.org/wp-content/uploads/2017/11/ASEAN-Statistical-Leaflet-2017_Final.pdf.

Asian Development Bank. 2017. "Accelerating Financial Inclusion in South-East Asia with Digital Finance." ADB.org. http://dx.doi.org/10.22617/RPT178622-2.

Athey, Susan, Ivo Parashkevov, Vishnu Sarukkai, and Jing Xia. 2016. "Bitcoin Pricing, Adoption, and Usage: Theory and Evidence." Stanford University Graduate School of Business Working Paper 3469. https://ssrn.com/abstract=2826674.

Auclert, Adrien. 2019. "Monetary Policy and the Redistribution Channel." *American Economic Review* 109 (6): 2333–2367.

Banerjee, Abhijit, Emily Breza, Robert M. Townsend, and Diego Vera-Cossio. 2018. "Access to Credit and Productivity: Evidence from Thai Villages." University of California, San Diego, Working Paper.

Bech, Morten, and Rodney Garratt. 2017. "Central Bank Cryptocurrencies." *BIS Quarterly Review* (September): 55–70. https://www.bis.org/publ/qtrpdf/r_qt1709f.pdf.

Bersem, Mario, Enrico Perotti, and Ernst-Ludwig von Thadden. 2013. "Sand in the Wheels of Capitalism: On the Political Economy of Capital Market Frictions." Copenhagen Business School Working Paper.

Bewley, Truman. 1983. "A Difficulty with the Optimum Quantity of Money." *Econometrica* 51(5): 1485–1504.

Bharadwaj, Prashant, William Jack, and Tavneet Suri. 2018. "Can Digital Loans Deliver? Take Up and Impacts of Digital Loans in Kenya." Working Paper.

Biais, Bruno, Christophe Bisiere, Matthieu Bouvard, Catherine Casamatta, and Albert Menkveld. 2018. "Equilibrium Bitcoin Pricing." Toulouse School of Economics Working Paper.

BIS (Bank for International Settlements). 2017a. "Distributed Ledger Technology in Payment, Clearing, and Settlement: An Analytical Framework." Committee on Payments and Market Infrastructures Paper No. 157 (February).

BIS (Bank for International Settlements). 2017b. "Distributed Ledgers in Payment, Clearing, and Settlement Carry Promise as Well as Risks." Press release, February 27. https://www.bis.org/press/p170227.htm.

BIS (Bank for International Settlements). 2018. "Cryptocurrencies: Looking beyond the Hype." *BIS Annual Economic Report* (June): 91–109. www.bis.org/publ/arpdf/ar2018e.htm.

Blockdata.tech. 2018. "Stablecoins: An Overview of the Current State of Stablecoins." https://download.blockdata.tech/blockdata-stablecoin-report-blockchain-technology.pdf.

Bronstein, Max. 2018. "Mapping the Decentralized Financial System: More Transparent, Open, and Programmable Financial Services." *MaxBronstein.com*, August 7. https://maxbronstein.com/mapping-the-decentralized-financial-system/.

Browning, Martin, Thomas F. Crossley, and Joachim Winter. 2014. "The Measurement of Household Consumption Expenditures." *Annual Review of Economics* 6 (6): 475–501.

Bryant, John, and Neil Wallace. 1984. "A Price Discrimination Analysis of Monetary Policy." *Review of Economic Studies* 51 (2): 279–288.

Budish, Eric. 2018. "The Economic Limits of Bitcoin and the Blockchain." University of Chicago Working Paper.

Budish, Eric, Peter Cramton, and John Shim. 2015. "The High-Frequency Trading Arms Race: Frequent Batch Auctions as a Market Design Response." *Quarterly Journal of Economics* 130 (4): 1547–1621.

Bureau of Economic Analysis. 2017. *NIPA Handbook: Concepts and Methods of the US National Income and Product Accounts.* US Department of Commerce (November). https://www.bea.gov/sites/default/files/methodologies/nipa-handbook-all-chapters.pdf.

Campbell-Kelly, Martin. 2010. "Victorian Data Processing." *Communications of the ACM* 53 (10): 19–21.

Cao, Sean S., Lin Cong, and Baozhong Yang. 2018. "Auditing and Blockchains: Pricing, Misstatements, and Regulation." Georgia State University Working Paper.

Carlson, Mark, Burcu Duygan-Bump, Fabio Natalucci, Bill Nelson, Marcelo Ochoa, and Jeremy Stein. 2016. "The Demand for Short-Term, Safe Assets and Financial Stability: Some Evidence and Implications for Central Bank Policies." *International Journal of Central Banking* 12 (4): 307–333.

Carlson, Stacy. 2017. "Essays in Financial Innovation and Development." PhD diss., MIT.

Casey, Michael, Jonah Crane, Gary Gensler, Simon Johnson, and Neha Narula. 2018. *The Impact of Blockchain Technology on Finance: A Catalyst for Change.* Vol. 21. Geneva Reports on the World Economy. Geneva: International Center for Monetary and Banking Studies. https://www.cimb.ch/uploads/1/1/5/4/115414161/geneva21_1.pdf.

Cass, David, Masahiro Okuno, and Itzhak Zilcha. 1978. "The Role of Money in Supporting the Pareto Optimality of Competitive Equilibrium in Consumption Loan Type Models." In *Models of Monetary Economies: Proceedings and Contributions from Participants of a December 1978 Conference*, 13–48. Minneapolis: Federal Reserve Bank of Minneapolis.

Chandrasekhar, Arun G., Robert M. Townsend, and Juan Pablo Xandri. 2018. "Financial Centrality and Liquidity Provision." MIT Working Paper.

Chen, Jing, Sergey Gorbunov, Silvio Micali, and Georgios Vlachos. 2018. "Algorand Agreement—Super Fast and Partition Resilient Byzantine Agreement." https://www.algorand.com/resources/white-papers/.

Chiappori, Pierre-André, Krislert Samphantharak, Sam Schulhofer-Wohl, and Robert M. Townsend. 2014. "Heterogeneity and Risk Sharing in Village Economies." *Quantitative Economics* 5 (1): 1–27.

Chiu, Jonathan, and Thorsten V. Koeppl. 2017. "The Economics of Cryptocurrencies—Bitcoin and Beyond." http://dx.doi.org/10.2139/ssrn.3048124.

Chwe, Michael Suk-Young. 1995. "Strategic Reliability of Communication Networks." University of Chicago Working Paper.

Cipolla, Carlo M. 1956. *Money, Prices, and Civilization in the Mediterranean World, Fifth to Seventeenth Century.* Princeton, NJ: Princeton University Press.

Clower, Robert. 1967. "A Reconsideration of the Microfoundations of Monetary Theory." *Economic Inquiry* 6 (1): 1–8.

Cocco, João F., Francisco J. Gomes, and Nuno C. Martins. 2009. "Lending Relationships in the Interbank Market." *Journal of Financial Intermediation* 18 (2009): 24–48.

Coles, Peter A., and Ran Shorrer. 2012. "Correlation in the Multiplayer Electronic Mail Game." *BE Journal of Theoretical Economics* 12 (1). doi:10.1515/1935-1704.1576.

Columbus, Louis. 2019. "Top 10 Ways Internet of Things and Blockchain Strengthen Supply Chains." *Forbes.com*, January 13. https://www.forbes.com/sites/louiscolumbus/2019/01/13/top-10-ways-internet-of-things-and-blockchain-strengthen-supply-chains/#4fea18ac5e4e.

Cong, Lin, Zhiguo He, and Jiasun Li. 2018. "Decentralized Mining in Centralized Pools." George Mason University School of Business Research Paper No. 18-9.

Cong, Lin William, and Zhiguo He. 2019. "Blockchain Disruption and Smart Contracts." *Review of Financial Studies* 32 (5): 1754–1797.

Crouzet, Nicolas, Apoorv Gupta, and Filippo Mezzanotti. 2019. "Shocks and Technology Adoption: Evidence from Electronic Payment Systems." Northwestern University Working Paper.

Curran, Brian. 2018. "What Is Practical Byzantine Fault Tolerance? Complete Beginner's Guide." *Blockonomi.com*, May 11. https://blockonomi.com/practical-byzantine-fault-tolerance/.

Dandekar, Pranav, Ashish Goel, Ramesh Govindan, and Ian Post. 2012. "Liquidity in Credit Networks: A Little Trust Goes a Long Way." Stanford University Working Paper.

Dasgupta, Partha, Peter Hammond, and Eric Maskin. 1979. "The Implementation of Social Choice Rules: Some General Results on Incentive Compatibility." *Review of Economic Studies* 46 (2): 185–216.

De, Nikhilesh. 2019. "Tether Lawyer Admits Stablecoin Now 74% Backed by Cash and Equivalents." *Coindesk*, May 1. https://www.coindesk.com/tether-lawyer-confirms-stablecoin-74-percent-backed-by-cash-and-equivalents.

De Jaegher, Kris, and Robert van Rooij. 2011. "Strategic Vagueness, and Appropriate Contexts." In *Language, Games, and Evolution*. Lecture Notes in Computer Science, Vol. 6207. Edited by A. Benz, C. Ebert, G. Jäger, and R. van Rooij. Berlin: Springer.

Denison, Erin, Michael Lee, and Antoine Martin. 2016. "What Do Cryptocurrencies Do?" Federal Reserve Bank of New York Conference Paper.

Diamond, Douglas W., and Philip H. Dybvig. 1983. "Bank Runs, Deposit Insurance, and Liquidity." *Journal of Political Economy* 91 (3): 401–419.

Diamond, Peter A. 1965. "National Debt in a Neoclassical Growth Model." *American Economic Review* 55 (5) Part 1: 1126–1150.

Doepke, Matthias, and Martin Schneider. 2006. "Inflation and the Redistribution of Nominal Wealth." *Journal of Political Economy* 114 (6): 1069–1097.

Doepke, Matthias, and Robert M. Townsend. 2006. "Dynamic Mechanism Design with Hidden Income and Hidden Actions." *Journal of Economic Theory*, 126 (1): 235–285.

Domeij, David, and Tore Ellingsen. 2018. "Monetary Policy in Incomplete Markets." Stockholm School of Economics Working Paper.

Du, Songzi, and Haoziang Zhu. 2017. "Are CDS Auctions Biased and Inefficient?" *Journal of Finance* 72: 2589–2628.

Duffie, Darrell, Nicolae Gârleanu, and Lasse Heje Pedersen. 2005. "Over-the-Counter Markets." *Econometrica* 73 (6): 1815–1847.

Erlandsson, Frida, and Gabriela Guibourg. 2018. "Times Are Changing and So Are Payment Patterns." Sveriges Riksbank Economic Commentaries No. 6 (May 14).

Falkon, Samuel. 2017. "The Story of the DAO—Its History and Consequences." *Medium.com*, December 24. https://medium.com/swlh/the-story-of-the-dao-its-history-and-consequences-71e6a8a551ee.

Fernandes, Ana, and Christopher Phelan. 2000. "A Recursive Formulation for Repeated Agency with History Dependence." *Journal of Economic Theory* 91 (2): 223–247.

Fernández-Villaverde, Jesús, and Daniel Sanches. 2016. "Can Currency Competition Work?" NBER Working Paper 22157.

Fischer, Michael J., Nancy A. Lynch, and Michael S. Paterson. 1985. "Impossibility of Distributed Consensus with One Faulty Process." *Journal of the Association for Computing Machinery* 32 (2): 374–382.

Foley, Sean, Jonathan R. Karlsen, and Talis J. Putnins. 2019. "Sex, Drugs, and Bitcoin: How Much Illegal Activity Is Financed through Cryptocurrencies?" *Review of Financial Studies* 32 (5): 1798–1853.

Freeman, Scott. 1996. "The Payments System, Liquidity, and Rediscounting." *American Economic Review* 86 (5): 1126–1138.

Fulford, Scott, and Scott Schuh. 2017. "Credit Card Utilization and Consumption over the Life Cycle and Business Cycle." Federal Reserve Bank of Boston Working Paper No. 17–14.

G20 Research Group. 2013. "The 2013 G20 St. Petersburg Summit Commitments." http://www.g20.utoronto.ca/analysis/commitments-13-stpetersburg.html.

Gale, Douglas, and Martin Hellwig. 1985. "Incentive-Compatible Debt Contracts: The One-Period Problem." *Review of Economic Studies* 52 (4): 647–663.

Gans, Joshua S. 2018. "The Fine Print in Smart Contracts." University of Toronto Working Paper.

Garratt, Rodney, Antoine Martin, Michael Junho Lee, and Robert M. Townsend. 2018. "Endogenous Liquidity and Interdealer Trading in Over-the-Counter Markets." Federal Reserve Bank of New York Working Paper.

Garratt, Rodney, and Neil Wallace. 2018. "Bitcoin 1, Bitcoin 2, … : An Experiment in Privately Issued Outside Monies." *Economic Inquiry* 56 (3): 1887–1897.

Geanakoplos, John. 2003. "Liquidity, Default, and Crashes, Endogenous Contracts in General Equilibrium." In *Advances in Economics and Econometrics: Theory and Applications, Eighth World Conference Volume II*, 170–205. Edited by M. Dewatripont, L. P. Hansen, and S. J. Turnovsky, Cambridge: Cambridge University Press.

Geerolf, François. 2017. "Reassessing Dynamic Efficiency." UCLA Working Paper.

Glazer, Phil. 2018. "Decentralized Cryptocurrency Exchanges." *BitcoinInsider.com*, March 6. https://www.bitcoininsider.org/article/19624/decentralized-cryptocurrency-exchanges.

Gord, Michael. 2016. "Smart Contracts Described by Nick Szabo 20 Years Ago Now Becoming Reality." *Bitcoin Magazine*, April 26. https://bitcoinmagazine.com/articles/smart-contracts-described-by-nick-szabo-years-ago-now-becoming-reality-1461693751.

Green, Edward J. 1987. "Lending and the Smoothing of Uninsurable Income." In *Contractual Arrangements for Intertemporal Trade*, 3–25. Edited by Edward C. Prescott and Neil Wallace. Minneapolis: University of Minnesota Press.

Green, Edward J. 1999. "Money and Debt in the Structure of Payments." *Federal Reserve Bank of Minneapolis Quarterly Review* 23 (Spring): 13–29.

Green, Edward J., and Ping Lin. 2003. "Implementing Efficient Allocations in a Model of Financial Intermediation," *Journal of Economic Theory* 109 (1): 1–23.

Green, Edward J., and Soo-Nam Oh. 1991. "Contracts, Constraints, and Consumption." *Review of Economic Studies* 58 (5): 883–899.

Green, Edward J., and Ruilin Zhou. 2005. "Money as a Mechanism in a Bewley Economy." *International Economic Review* 46 (2): 351–371.

Greenwood, Robin, Samuel G. Hanson, and Jeremy C. Stein. 2016. "The Federal Reserve's Balance Sheet as a Financial-Stability Tool." In *2016 Economic Policy Symposium Proceedings*. Jackson Hole: Federal Reserve Bank of Kansas City.

Griffin, John, and Amin Shams. 2018. "Is Bitcoin Really Un-Tethered?" University of Texas at Austin Working Paper.

Güntzer, Michael M., Dieter Jungnickel, and Matthias Leclerc. 1998. "Efficient Algorithms for the Clearing of Interbank Payments." *European Journal of Operational Research* 106 (1): 212–219.

Halpern, Joseph Y., and Yoram Moses. 1990. "Knowledge and Common Knowledge in a Distributed Environment." *Journal of the Association for Computing Machinery* 37 (3): 549–587.

Harford, Tim. 2017. "What Tally Sticks Tell Us about How Money Works." *BBC.com*, July 10. https://www.bbc.com/news/business-40189959.

Harris, Milton, and Artur Raviv. 1979. "Optimal Incentive Contracts with Imperfect Information." *Journal of Economic Theory* 20 (2): 231–259.

Harris, Milton, and Robert M. Townsend. 1981. "Resource Allocation under Asymmetric Information." *Econometrica* 49 (1): 33–64.

Hart, Oliver, and John Moore. 2007. "Incomplete Contracts and Ownership: Some New Thoughts." *American Economic Review* 97 (2): 182–186.

Helix Institute of Digital Finance. 2017. "Agent Network Accelerator Research: Indonesia Country Report." https://www.microsave.net/wp-content/uploads/2018/12/ANA-Indonesia.pdf.

Hendershott, Terrence, and Ananth Madhavan. 2015. "Click or Call: Auction vs. Search in the OTC Market." *Journal of Finance* 70 (1): 419–447.

Hinzen, Franz J., Kose John, and Fahad Saleh. 2019. "Proof-of-Work's Limited Adoption Problem." NYU Stern School of Business Working Paper.

Holden, Richard, and Anup Malani. 2018. "Can Blockchains Solve the Holdup Problem in Contracts?" Becker-Friedman Institute, University of Chicago, Working Paper No. 2018-12.

Huggett, Mark, and Greg Kaplan. 2015. "How Large Is the Stock Component of Human Capital?" NBER Working Paper 21238.

Hussam, Reshmaan, Natalia Rigol, and Benjamin Roth. 2017. "Targeting High Ability Entrepreneurs Using Community Information: Mechanism Design in the Field." Harvard University Working Paper.

Iansiti, Marco, and Karim R. Lakhani. 2017. "The Truth about Blockchain." *Harvard Business Review* 95 (1): 118–127.

IBM. 2019. "Hyperledger Fabric: The Flexible Blockchain Framework That's Changing the Business World," https://www.ibm.com/blockchain/hyperledger.

Ingves, Stefan. 2016. "Efficient Payment Systems and the Riksbank's Approach to Cash Distribution." Money and Banking Conference, Central Bank of Argentina.

Inveniam Capital Partners. 2019. "Update: WeWork, NDSU Housing, Cape at Savona, Impact Africa, and Takenization." YouTube video, 39:16, June 19. https://www.youtube.com/watch?v=DEsQegxLjBk.

IPFS. 2019. "IPFS Powers the Distributed Web." https://ipfs.io/.

Jack, William, and Tavneet Suri. 2011. "Mobile Money: The Economics of M-PESA." NBER Working Paper No. 16721.

Jack, William, and Tavneet Suri. 2014. "Risk Sharing and Transactions Costs: Evidence from Kenya's Mobile Money Revolution." *American Economic Review*, 104 (1): 183–223.

Jack, William, Tavneet Suri, and Robert M. Townsend. 2010. "Monetary Theory and Electronic Money: Reflections on the Kenyan Experience." *Economic Quarterly* 96 (1): 83–122.

Jacklin, Charles J. 1987. "Demand Deposits, Trading Restrictions, and Risk Sharing." In *Contractual Arrangements for Intertemporal Trade*, 26–47. Edited by Edward C. Prescot and Neil Wallace. Minneapolis: University of Minnesota Press.

Janin, Simon, Arthur Gervais, and Akaki Mamageishvili. 2019. "FileBounty: Secure and Efficient File Exchange in a Rational Adversarial Environment." ETH Zurich Working Paper.

Joaquim, Gustavo, Robert M. Townsend, and Victor Zhorin. 2018. "Optimal Contracting and Imperfect Competition among Financial Service Providers." MIT Working Paper.

Kaboski, Joseph P., and Robert M. Townsend. 2011. "A Structural Evaluation of Large-Scale Quasi-experimental Microfinance Initiative." *Econometrica* 79 (5): 1357–1406.

Kaboski, Joseph P., and Robert M. Townsend. 2012. "The Impact of Credit on Village Economies." *American Economic Journal: Applied Economics* 4 (2): 98–133.

Kaplan, Greg, and Giovanni L. Violante. 2014. "A Model of the Consumption Response to Fiscal Stimulus Payments." *Econometrica* 82 (4): 1199–1239.

Karaivanov, Alexander, and Robert M. Townsend. 2014. "Dynamic Financial Constraints: Distinguishing Mechanism Design from Exogenously Incomplete Regimes." *Econometrica* 82 (3): 887–959.

Kareken, John, and Neil Wallace. 1981. "On the Indeterminacy of Equilibrium Exchange Rates." *Quarterly Journal of Economics* 96 (2): 207–222.

Kehoe, Timothy J., David K. Levine, and Michael Woodford. 1990. "The Optimum Quantity of Money Revisited." Federal Reserve Bank of Minneapolis Working Paper 404.

Kestenbaum, David. 2012. "The Accountant Who Changed the World." *All Things Considered*, National Public Radio (NPR), broadcast October 4.

Kilenthong, Weerachart T., and Robert M. Townsend. 2018. "A Market Based Solution for Fire Sales and Other Pecuniary Externalities." MIT Working Paper.

Kim, Kyungmin. 2015. "Summary of 'Money and the Decentralization of Exchange' and Some Comments." Board of Governors of the Federal Reserve System Working Paper.

Kimberley, David. 2019. "MAS and Bank of Canada Complete Blockchain Payments Test." *Finance Magnates*, February 5. https://www.financemagnates.com/fintech/payments/mas-and-bank-of-canada-complete-blockchain-payments-test.

Kinnan, Cynthia, Krislert Samphantharak, Robert M. Townsend, and Diego Vera-Cossio. 2018. "Networks and Risk Sharing in Village Economies." MIT Working Paper.

Kinnan, Cynthia, and Robert Townsend. 2012. "Kinship and Financial Networks, Formal Financial Access, and Risk Reduction." *American Economic Review* 102 (3): 289–293.

Klein, Benjamin. 1976. "Competing Monies: Comment." *Journal of Money* 8 (4): 512–519.

Kocherlakota, Narayana R. 1998. "Money Is Memory." *Journal of Economic Theory* 81 (2): 232–251.

Krishnamurthy, Arvind, and Annette Vissing-Jorgensen. 2012. "The Aggregate Demand for Treasury Debt." *Journal of Political Economy* 120 (2): 233–267.

Kuussaari, Harri. 1996. "Systemic Risk in the Finnish Payment System: An Empirical Investigation." Bank of Finland Discussion Paper No. 3/96.

Lagos, Ricardo, and Randall Wright. 2005. "A Unified Framework for Theory and Policy Analysis." *Journal of Political Economy* 113 (3): 463–484.

Lagos, Ricardo, and Shengxing Zhang. 2018. "Turnover Liquidity and the Transmission of Monetary Policy." Federal Reserve Bank of Minneapolis Working Paper No. 734.

Lamport, Leslie, Robert Shostak, and Marshall Pease. 1982. "The Byzantine Generals Problem." *ACM Transactions on Programming Languages and Systems* 4 (3): 382–401.

Lehnert, Andreas, Ethan Ligon, and Robert M. Townsend. 1999. "Liquidity Constraints and Incentive Contracts." *Macroeconomic Dynamics* 3 (1): 1–47.

Leong, Nicholas. 2017. "Remittances Are Ripping Off Migrant Workers in ASEAN." *EastAsiaForum.org*, reposted to Eaber.org. November 8. http://www.eaber.org/node/26610.

Levine, David K. 1989. "Efficiency and the Value of Money." *Review of Economic Studies* 56 (1): 77–88.

Li, Dan, and Norman Schürhoff. 2012. "Dealer Networks: Market Quality in Over-the-Counter Markets." Federal Reserve Bank of New York Working Paper.

Ligon, Ethan, Jonathan P. Thomas, and Tim Worrall. 2002. "Informal Insurance Arrangements with Limited Commitment: Theory and Evidence from Village Economies." *Review of Economic Studies* 69 (1): 209–244.

Lim, Youngjae, and Robert M. Townsend. 1998. "General Equilibrium Models of Financial Systems: Theory and Measurement in Village Economies." *Review of Economic Dynamics* 1 (1): 59–118.

Lucas, Robert E., and Nancy L. Stokey. 1983. "Optimal Fiscal and Monetary Policy in an Economy without Capital." *Journal of Monetary Economics* 12 (1): 55–93.

Lumenauts.com. 2018. "How the Stellar Consensus Protocol (Federated Byzantine Agreement) Works." YouTube video, 9:43, April 18. https://www.youtube.com/watch?v=X3Gj2nQZCNM.

Lyon, Richard K. 1996. "Optimal Transparency in a Dealer Market with an Application to Foreign Exchange." *Journal of Financial Intermediation*, 5 (3): 225–254.

Makerdao.com. 2017. "The Dai Stablecoin System." White Paper (December). https://makerdao.com/whitepaper/Dai-Whitepaper-Dec17-en.pdf.

Makerdao.com. 2019. "Dai 1.0: Introduction, Stability, Core, CLI, Query API." https://developer.makerdao.com/dai/1/

Makowski, Louis. 1980. "A Characterization of Perfectly Competitive Economies with Production," *Journal of Economic Theory* 22 (2): 208–221.

Mallett, Jacky. 2009. "Limits on the Communication of Knowledge in Human Organisations." *Studies in Emergent Order* 2: 1–18.

Mallett, Jacky. 2019. Personal correspondence, January.

Manuelli, Rodolfo, and Thomas J. Sargent. 1988. "Longer Trading Periods in a Townsend Turnpike Model." Stanford University Working Paper.

Manuelli, Rodolfo, and Thomas J. Sargent. 2010. "Alternative Monetary Policies in a Turnpike Economy." *Macroeconomic Dynamics* 14 (5): 727–762.

Martin, Antoine, Michael Lee, and Robert Townsend. 2017. Personal correspondence, December.

Martin, Antoine, and James McAndrews. 2008. "An Economic Analysis of Liquidity-Saving Mechanism." *Economic Policy Review* 14 (2): 25–39.

Martin, Antoine, David Skeie, and Ernst-Ludwig von Thadden. 2013. "The Fragility of Short-term Secured Funding Markets." Federal Reserve Bank of New York Staff Reports No. 630.

Martin, Antoine, David Skeie, and Ernst-Ludwig von Thadden. 2014. "Repo Runs." *Review of Financial Studies* 27 (4): 957–989.

Maskin, Eric, and Jean Tirole. 1999. "Unforeseen Contingencies and Incomplete Contracts." *Review of Economic Studies* 66 (1): 83–114.

Mazieres, David. 2016. "The Stellar Consensus Protocol: A Federated Model for Internet-level Consciousness." *Stellar.org*, February 25. https://assets.website-files.com/5deac75ecad2173c2cccbc7/5df2560fba2fb0526f0ed55f_stellar-consensus-protocol.pdf.

McAndrews, James, and William Roberds. 1999. "Payment Intermediation and the Origins of Banking." Federal Reserve Bank of Atlanta Working Paper No. 99–11.

Miller, Merton H., and Daniel Orr. 1966. "A Model of the Demand for Money by Firms." *Quarterly Journal of Economics* 80: 413–435.

Mills, David, Kathy Wang, Brendan Malone, Anjana Ravi, Jeff Marquardt, Clinton Chen, Anton Badev, Timothy Brezinski, Linda Fahy, Kimberley Liao, Vanessa Kargenian, Max Ellithorpe, Wendy Ng, and Maria Baird. 2016. "Distributed Ledger Technology in Payments, Clearing, and Settlement." Federal Reserve Board Finance and Economics Discussion Series No. 2016–095.

Monetary Authority of Singapore. 2018. "Cross-Border Interbank Payments and Settlements: Emerging Opportunities for Digital Transformation." Project Report. Accessed March 22, 2019. https://www.mas.gov.sg/-/media/MAS/ProjectUbin/Cross-Border-Interbank-Payments-and-Settlements.pdf.

Monetary Authority of Singapore and the Association of Banks in Singapore. 2017. "Project Ubin Phase 2: Re-imagining Interbank Real-Time Gross Settlement System Using Distributed Ledger Technologies." Accessed November 15, 2018. https://www.accenture.com/t20171116T081243Z__w__/sg-en/_acnmedia/PDF-66/Accenture-Project-Ubin-Phase-2.pdf.

Monnet, Cyril, and Thomas Nellen. 2014. "The Collateral Costs of Clearing." Swiss National Bank (SNB) Working Paper 4/2014.

Moore, John. 1992. "Implementation, Contracts, and Renegotiation in Environments with Complete Information." In *Advances in Economic Theory: Sixth World Congress, Volume 1*, 182–282. Edited by Jean-Jacques Laffont. Cambridge: Cambridge University Press.

Moore, John, and Rafael Repullo. 1988. "Subgame Perfect Implementation," *Econometrica* 56 (5): 1191–1220.

Moore, John, and Rafael Repullo. 1990. "Nash Implementation: A Full Characterization." *Econometrica* 58 (5): 1083–1099.

Morris, David Z. 2019. "Tether Now Admits It's Not Fully Backed by Dollars." *Breakermag*, March 14. https://breakermag.com/tether-now-admits-its-not-fully-backed-by-dollars/.

Morris, Stephen, and Hyun Song Shin. 1997. "Approximate Common Knowledge and Co-ordination: Recent Lessons from Game Theory." *Journal of Logic, Language, and Information* 6: 171–190.

Moskov, Phillip. 2018. "What Is Bit Gold? The Brainchild of Blockchain Pioneer Nick Szabo." *Coincentral.com*, May 22. https://coincentral.com/what-is-bit-gold-the-brainchild-of-blockchain-pioneer-nick-szabo/.

Muley, Ameya. 2016. "Collateral Reuse in Shadow Banking and Monetary Policy." MIT Job Market Paper.

Myerson, Roger B. 1982. "Optimal Coordination Mechanisms in Generalized Principal-Agent Problems." *Journal of Mathematical Economics* 10 (1): 67–81.

Myerson, Roger B. 1986. "Multistage Games with Communication." *Econometrica* 54 (2): 323–358.

Nakamoto, Satoshi. 2008. "Bitcoin: A Peer-to-Peer Electronic Cash System." White Paper. Accessed October 28, 2018. https://bitcoin.org/bitcoin.pdf.

Narayanan, Arvind, Joseph Bonneau, Edward Felten, Andrew Miller, and Steven Goldfeder. 2016. *Bitcoin and Cryptocurrency Technologies: A Comprehensive Introduction*. Princeton, NJ: Princeton University Press.

Narayanan, Arvind, and Matt Weinberg. 2018. "Survey of Algorithmic Game Theory Research Questions for Crypto/Blockchain." Lecture presented at "Cryptocurrencies and Blockchains," Becker-Friedman Institute, University of Chicago, November.

Ostroy, Joseph M., and Ross M. Starr. 1974. "Money and the Decentralization of Exchange." *Econometrica* 42 (6): 1093–1113.

Palfrey, Thomas R., and Sanjay Srivastava. 1989. "Mechanism Design with Incomplete Information: A Solution to the Implementation Problem." *Journal of Political Economy* 97 (3): 668–691.

Paweenawat, Archawa, and Robert M. Townsend. 2012. "Village Economic Accounts: Real and Financial Intertwined." *American Economics Review* 102 (3): 441–446.

Paweenawat, Archawa, and Robert M. Townsend. 2018. "The Impact of Regional Isolationism: Disentangling Real and Financial Factors." MIT Working Paper.

Payments Canada. 2017. "Project Jasper: A Canadian Experiment with Distributed Ledger Technology for Domestic Interbank Payments Settlement." Payments Canada, Bank of Canada, and R3 White Paper (September 29). Accessed on October 19, 2018. https://www.payments.ca/sites/default/files/29-Sep-17/jasper_report_eng.pdf.

Pesendorfer, Wolfgang. 1995. "Financial Innovation in a General Equilibrium Model." *Journal of Economic Theory* 65 (1): 79–116.

Phelan, Christopher, and Robert M. Townsend. 1991. "Computing Multiperiod Information Constrained Optima." *Review of Economic Studies* 58 (5): 853–883.

Piazzesi, Monika, and Martin Schneider. 2018. "Payments, Credit, and Asset Prices." Stanford University Working Paper.

Prat, Julien, and Benjamin Walter. 2018. "An Equilibrium Model of the Market for Bitcoin Mining." École Polytechnique Working Paper.

Prescott, Edward C., and Robert M. Townsend. 1984a. "Pareto Optima and Competitive Equilibria with Adverse Selection and Moral Hazard." *Econometrica* 52 (1): 21–45.

Prescott, Edward C., and Robert M. Townsend. 1984b. "General Competitive Analysis in an Economy with Private Information." International Economic Review 25 (1): 1–20.

Prescott, Edward S. 2003. "Communication in Private-Information Models: Theory and Computation." *Geneva Papers on Risk and Insurance Theory* 28 (2): 105–130.

Prescott, Edward S., and Robert M. Townsend. 2006a. "Firms as Clubs in Walrasian Markets with Private Information." Journal of Political Economy 114 (4): 644–671.

Prescott, Edward S., and Robert M. Townsend. 2006b. "Private Information and Intertemporal Job Assignments." *Review of Economic Studies* 73 (2): 531–548.

Ray, Shaan. 2017. "Blockchains versus Traditional Databases." *Emerging Technology Blog, HackerNoon.com*, November 5. https://hackernoon.com/blockchains-versus-traditional-databases-c1a7281 59f79.

Ray, Shaan. 2018. "Federated Byzantine Agreement." *Emerging Technology Blog, TowardsDataScience.com*, April 8. https://towardsdatascience.com/federated-byzantine-agreement-24ec57bf36e0.

Reese, Frederick. 2017. "Land Registry: A Big Blockchain Explored." *CoinDesk*, April 19. www.coindesk.com/blockchain-land-registry-solution-seeking-problem/.

Roberts, John Jeff. "Facebook's Project Libra: 5 Things to Know about the Cryptocurrency." *Fortune*, June 18. https://fortune.com/2019/06/18/facebook-project-libra-crypto-coin-cryptocurrency-how-it-works/.

Robinson, Henry. 2009. "Barbara Liskov's Turing Award, and Byzantine Fault Tolerance." *The Paper Trail Blog*, March 30. https://www.the-paper-trail.org/post/2009-03-30-barbara-liskovs-turing-award-and-byzantine-fault-tolerance/.

Rogoff, Kenneth S. 2016. *The Curse of Cash*. Princeton, NJ: Princeton University Press.

Roth, Benjamin N., and Ran I. Shorrer. 2017. "Making It Safe to Use Centralized Marketplaces: Dominant Individual Rationality and Applications to Market Design." Harvard Business School Working Paper.

Ru, Hong, and Robert M. Townsend. 2018. "Narrowing the GAP: The Costly State Verification Regime in Rural Thailand." MIT Working Paper.

Rubinstein, Ariel. 1989. "The Electronic Mail Game: Strategic Behavior under 'Almost Common Knowledge.'" *American Economic Review* 79 (3): 385–391.

Samphantharak, Krislert, Scott Schuh, and Robert M. Townsend. 2016. "Integrated Household Surveys: An Assessment of US Methods and an Innovation." Federal Reserve Bank of Boston Working Paper.

Samphantharak, Krislert, and Robert M. Townsend. 2009. *Households as Corporate Firms: An Analysis of Household Finance Using Integrated Constructing Financial Statements from Integrated*

*Household Surveys and Corporate Financial Accounting*. Econometric Society Monograph Series. Cambridge: Cambridge University Press.

Samphantharak, Krislert, and Robert M. Townsend. 2018. "Risk and Return in Village Economies." *American Economic Journal-Microeconomics* 10 (1): 1–40.

Samuelson, Paul A. 1958. "An Exact Consumption-Loan Model of Interest with or without the Social Contrivance of Money." *Journal of Political Economy* 66 (6): 467–482.

Schilling, L., and Harald Uhlig. 2018. "Some Simple Bitcoin Economics." Becker Friedman Institute for Research in Economics Working Paper No. 2018-21.

Schmandt-Besserat, Denise. 2014. "Tokens: Their Significance for the Origin of Counting and Writing." *UTexas.edu*. Accessed January 29, 2019. https://sites.utexas.edu/dsb/tokens/tokens/.

Schuh, Scott, and Joanna Stavins. 2014. "The 2011 and 2012 Surveys of Consumer Payment Choice." Federal Reserve Bank of Boston Research Data Report No. 14–1.

Schuster, Brian. 2017. "The Ripple Currency Problem: Why Permissioned Blockchains Will Devalue XRP." *Hackernoon.com*, December 4. https://hackernoon.com/the-ripple-currency-problem-why-permissioned-blockchains-will-devalue-xrp-d79aef84c074.

Sharma, Toshendra Kumar. 2019. "Quorum vs. Hyperledger: The Ultimate Guide." Blockchain Council, May 15. https://www.blockchain-council.org/hyperledger/quorum-vs-hyperledger-the-ultimate-guide/.

Shin, Hyun Song. 2018. "Cryptocurrencies and the Economics of Money." Speech given at Bank for International Settlements, Annual General Meeting, Basel, June 24.

Singh, Manmohan. 2011. "Velocity of Pledged Collateral: Analysis and Implications." International Monetary Fund Working Paper.

Skingsley, Cecilia. 2016. "Should the Riksbank Issue e-Krona?" Lecture presented at FinTech Stockholm/Berns, Sweden, November 16.

Spear, Stephen E., and Sanjay Srivastava. 1987. "On Repeated Moral Hazard with Discounting." *Review of Economic Studies* 54 (4): 599–617.

Spector, Mariano, and Robert Townsend. 2019. "Notes on the Townsend Wallace Coordination Problem." MIT Research Notes.

Sprague, Oliver M. W. 1910. "History of Crises under the National Banking System." National Monetary Commission (1910 [1968]), 51st Cong., 2nd Sess., Senate Document No. 538.

Sripakdeevong, Parit, and Robert M. Townsend. 2018. "The Village Money Market Revealed: Credit Chains and Shadow Banking." MIT Working Paper.

Starr, Ross M. 1974. "The Price of Money in a Pure Exchange Monetary Economy with Taxation," *Econometrica* 42 (1): 45–54.

Suri, Tavneet. 2017. "Mobile Money." *Annual Review of Economics* 9: 497–520.

Sveriges Riksbank. 2018. "Payment Patterns in Sweden 2018." *Riksbank.se* (May). https://www.riksbank.se/globalassets/media/statistik/betalningsstatistik/2018/payments-patterns-in-sweden-2018.pdf.

Swedish Post and Telecom Authority. 2017. "Grundläggande betaltjänster i en digitaliserad framtid [Essential Payment Services in a Digitalised Future]." Swedish Post and Telecom Authority Report No. PTS-ER-2017:20 (December 1). https://www.pts.se/globalassets/startpage/dokument/icke-legala-dokument/rapporter/2017/post/grundlaggande-betaltjanster-i-en-digitaliserad-framtid---pts-er-2017_20.pdf.

Szabo, Nick. 1998. "Secure Property Titles with Owner Authority." Satoshi Nakamoto Institute. Accessed February 19, 2019. https://nakamotoinstitute.org/secure-property-titles/.

Tirole, Jean. 1985. "Asset Bubbles and Overlapping Generations." *Econometrica* 53 (6): 1499–1528.

Tobin, James. 1978. "Discussion." In *Models of Monetary Economies: Proceedings and Contributions from Participants of a December 1978 Conference*, 83–90. Minneapolis: Federal Reserve Bank of Minneapolis.

Townsend, Robert M. 1977. "The Eventual Failure of Price Fixing Schemes." *Journal of Economic Theory* 14 (3): 190–199.

Townsend, Robert M. 1978. "Intermediation with Costly Bilateral Exchange." *Review of Economic Studies* 45 (3): 417–425.

Townsend, Robert M. 1979. "Optimal Contracts and Competitive Markets with Costly State Verification." *Journal of Economic Theory* 21 (2): 265–293.

Townsend, Robert M. 1980. "Models of Money with Spatially Separated Agents." In *Models of Monetary Economies*, 265–303. Edited by John Kareken and Neil Wallace. Minneapolis: Federal Reserve Bank of Minneapolis.

Townsend, Robert M. 1982. "Optimal Multiperiod Contracts and the Gain from Enduring Relationships under Private Information." *Journal of Political Economy* 90 (6): 1166–1186.

Townsend, Robert M. 1987. "Economic Organization with Limited Communication." *American Economic Review* 77 (5): 954–971.

Townsend, Robert M. 1988. "Information Constrained Insurance: The Revelation Principle Extended." *Journal of Monetary Economics* 21 (2/3): 411–450.

Townsend, Robert M. 1989. "Currency and Credit in a Private Information Economy." *Journal of Political Economy* 97 (6): 1323–1344.

Townsend, Robert M. 1990. *Financial Structure and Economic Organization*. Cambridge, MA: Blackwell.

Townsend, Robert M. 2016. "Village and Larger Economies: The Theory and Measurement of the Townsend Thai Project." *Journal of Economic Perspectives* 30 (4): 199–220.

Townsend, Robert M. 2019. "Online Appendix: Distributed Ledgers." http://www.robertmtownsend.net/research/online-appendix.

Townsend, Robert M., and Neil Wallace. 1987. "Circulating Private Debt: An Example with a Coordination Problem." In *Contractual Arrangements for Intertemporal Trade*. Edited by Edward C. Prescott and Neil Wallace. Minneapolis: University of Minnesota Press.

Townsend, Robert, and Juan Pablo Xandri. 2018. "Regulation and the Optimal Design of Financial Markets." MIT Working Paper.

Townsend Thai Project. 2019. In cooperation with the National Bureau of Economic Research. http://townsend-thai.mit.edu/.

Trubek, Anne. 2015. "What the Heck Is Cuneiform, Anyway?" *SmithsonianMag.com*, October 20. https://www.smithsonianmag.com/history/what-heck-cuneiform-anyway-180956999/#dcLC5HSIETSzgobb.03.

Tucker, Paul. 2014. "Are Clearing Houses the New Central Banks?" Over-the-Counter Derivatives Symposium, Chicago.

u/PumpkinFeet. 2018. "What Is the Difference between Normal Byzantine Fault Tolerance and Practical BFT, Asynchronous BFT, Delegated BFT etc.? And Which Coins Use Which One? How Do They Relate to PoW and PoS etc?" *Reddit*, r/CrytoTechnology. https://

www.reddit.com/r/CryptoTechnology/comments/8782mb/what_is_the_difference_between_normal_byzantine/.

Vera-Cossio, Diego A. 2018. "Targeting Credit through Community Members." University of California, San Diego, Working Paper.

Wallace, Neil. 2014. "Optimal Money Creation in 'Pure Currency' Economies: A Conjecture." *Quarterly Journal of Economics* 129 (1): 259–274.

Wikipedia. 2018a. "Informal Value Transfer System." Accessed November 6, 2018. https://en.wikipedia.org/w/index.php?title=Informal_value_transfer_system&oldid=840911091.

Wikipedia. 2018b. "Distributed Data Store." Accessed November 19, 2018. https://en.wikipedia.org/wiki/Distributed_data_store.

Wikipedia. 2019a. "CAP Theorem." Accessed November 17, 2019. https://en.wikipedia.org/wiki/CAP_theorem.

Wikipedia. 2019b. "Synchronization (Computer Science)." Accessed January 28, 2019. https://en.wikipedia.org/wiki/Synchronization.

Woodford, Michael. 1990. "Public Debt as Private Liquidity." *American Economic Review* 80 (2): 382–388.

Xandri, Juan Pablo. 2016. "Credible Reforms: A Robust Implementation Approach." Princeton University Working Paper.

XRP Ledger. 2019. "Run a Rippled Validator." https://xrpl.org/run-a-rippled-validator.html.

Zhang, Nicolas. 2019. Personal correspondence, August.

# Index

Accrual income method, 39
Agents, 24, 185n1
  in Ostroy-Starr model, 138–139
  small and medium-sized enterprises as, 25
  smart contracts and, 25, 26, 80
  waterfall payment and, 119
Agrello, 94
AirSwap, 58
Algorand, 16, 75
Alibaba/Ant Financial, 89
Allocations, 12, 24
Amazon Cloud, 44
Anchors, in Stellar, 74–75, 149
Asian Development Bank, 115, 174
Asset-backed off-chain, 160–161
Asset-backed on-chain, 161
Assets, 74, 93
Association of Banks, in Singapore, 184n3
Association of Southeast Asian Nations (ASEAN), 116
Asynchronous systems, 14, 46

Auctions, collusion and, 92
Auditor, role of, 112–113
Australian Stock Exchange, Digital Asset and, 37, 46
Autarky, 159, 178
Availability, distributed ledgers and, 44–45
Axoni, 7

Backing mechanisms, cryptocurrency, 160–163, 179
Back-loading, 107, 174
Balance of payments accounts, village financial accounts and, 40–41
Balance sheet, 27
  changes in income statement and, 39
  creation of financial statements and, 38
  cryptocurrency on, 38
  items on, 38
  as a ledger, 31–38
  in village economies, 31, 32–33, 36
Banishment penalty, 90
Bankers Clearing House, 13

Bank for International Settlements, 2, 3, 181n5
Bankgirot system, 52
Bank of Canada, 127, 128, 129, 175–176
Bank of England, 129
Banks. *See also* Central banks
  digital reserve, 20, 163–165
  mitigating runs on, 133–135
Bargaining, 94
Base account, in Stellar, 74
Bayesian Nash equilibrium, 81, 92, 134
Bills of exchange, 143, 149
Binance, 58
Bitcoin
  absence of central authority, 9
  bubble in, 159
  coloring coins and, 184n3
  controversy over, 178
  distributed ledger technology, blockchain, and, 1
  double-spending and, 68, 70
  encryption and, 68–71
  as innovation or invention, 4, 10
  miners and, 67, 68–70
  proof of work and, 65–66, 67, 171
  security and, 44
  two keys to, 69
  user fees for, 181n5
  validation and, 8, 77
Bitcoin cryptography, 16
Bitfinex, 161
Bit gold, 10
Blockchain protocol, proof-of-work, modeled as stochastic game, 70

Blockchains, 1
  contracts and, 2–3
  permissioned or private, 46–47
  resolution of hold-up problem in, 92–93
  security and, 44
  smart contracts and, 67
Blockdata.tech, 160
Bond market, 153
Broker-dealers, e-money shortages and, 56–58
Bubbles, 159, 179
Bureau of Economic Analysis, 40
Byzantine Agreement, 66
Byzantine Fault Toleration (BFT), 16, 66, 67
Byzantine Generals Problem, 65, 79, 98–102

Canada, Project Jasper, 20, 127–129, 175–176
CAP (consistency, availability, partition tolerance) theorem, 44–45, 46
Capital One, 44
Cash flow method, 39
Cash flow statement, 27
  creation of financial statements and, 38
  as a ledger, 31, 35, 36
  similarities/differences with income statement, 38–39
  for United States, 42
Cash in advance, value of money and, 156–157
Cash mismanagement, cost of, 51
Cash transactions, recorded on ledgers, 31, 36

Cell phone credits, M-Pesa and, 54–55, 56
Central banks
  cashless society and, 51–52
  commitments and, 163
  cryptocurrencies and, 181n5
  mitigation of moral-hazard problem and, 135
  motives for trade and, 140
  payments and, 3
  smoothing interest rate, 165
Central counterparty (CCP) clearing, 184n3
Centralization
  delegation of portfolios to third party and, 105–107
  Fischer Consensus Problem and, 46
  smart contract and, 79
Centralized platforms, 47
Central warehouse, 140
Certification in Bitcoin, 69
Checks, paper, 148, 149
China, regulation of delegation to platforms, 184n1
Clearing House of New York, 13
Coding costs, 94–97
Coinbase, 58
Coins. *See also* Tokens
  coloring, 184n3
  histories of, 18, 111
  stable, 160–163, 179
Collateral, 93, 119, 141
Collateralized debt positions (CDPs), 161–162
Collusion, 92, 122, 172
Coloring coins, 184n3. *See also* Multiple colored tokens

Commitment
  built into communication protocol, 101
  in cryptocurrency design, 163
  in economics, 94
Commitment savings accounts, 120
Committee on Payments and Market Infrastructures (CPMI), 3
Commodity space of an economy, 123
Communication
  fixed objective and naive, 99–100, 101
  under smart contract, 79
Communication systems, optimal design of, 17–18
Community-level financial accounts, 40–41
Competition
  among distributed ledger providers, 20–21
  limiting, for smart contracts, 135–137
Complete-markets equilibrium real allocation, 141–142
Complexity, novelty *vs.*, 3
Computer science
  economics *vs.*, 17
  smart contracts in, 93–102
  synchronization in, 45
Concealment, partitioned ledgers and, 104–106
Conditionality, savings products and, 120
Consensus
  asynchronous systems and, 14
  Byzantine Generals Problem and, 65

Consensus (cont.)
  differences among protocols, 65–68
  distributed, 64–68
  e-systems and, 15–16
  permissioned private ledgers and lack of unique, 111–113
  regulation and, 177
  on shared distributed ledger, 37
  unique, 78, 108–109
  validity, 78
Consensus algorithms, 16
  blockchain platforms and, 67–68
Consensus categorization, 40, 168
Consistency, distributed ledgers and, 44–45
Constrained-optimal contract, 84, 85–86, 104
Constrained-optimal solutions, 13
Constraints, economic, 24
Context, innovation and, 4
Contract competition, 175, 177
Contract node as planner, 173–174
Contracts. *See also* Smart contracts
  blockchain and, 2–3
  distributed ledger technology and, 13–14
  money and, 25
  to purchase and sale of commodity or asset, 89
  time line of events within given period under, 27, 28
Coordination, circulating private debt and, 141–142, 143

Corda
  latency and, 45
  notary service on, 80
  as permissioned ledger system, 66, 67
  Project Jasper and, 127, 128
  smart contracts and, 6, 68, 77–78, 79
  tokens and, 112
  unique consensus and, 121
Cost
  of cash mismanagement, 51
  of coding and implementation of smart contracts, 94–97
  of decentralization, 173
  transaction, 24
Costly state verification, 88
Credit, 140, 148
Credit cards, 52, 148
Credit derivatives, 7
Cross-border payments
  Lightnet and Velo and, 130–132
  Project Jasper and, 129
Crossley, Thomas F., 43
CRUD (create, read, update, or delete), 44
Cryptocurrencies, 21–22, 59, 145–165. *See also* Bitcoin
  on balance sheet, 38
  central banks and, 181n5
  fiat money and, 178–179
  hybrid model of positive token values, 157–158
  incentives for compliance in, 94
  interest rate policy for digital reserve bank, 163–165
  as means of payment, 149–150

mechanism design for tokens and, 150–151
as media of exchange, 147–148
monetary theory in Walrasian competitive markets and, 151–156
multiple media, 148–150, 178
need for commitment in design, 163
number of, 8, 181n3
stable coins, 160–163
tokens and, 145–146, 157–158
value of money and, 156–160
Cryptocurrency exchanges, 11, 58
Cryptographic hash, 97
Cryptography, 13, 170–171
CSD (clearing house), 37
Currency. *See also* Paper currency
elastic, 164–165
ghost, 150
Currency infrastructure, in Sweden, 182n1
Currency to GDP ratio, 49, 52, 169
Custodians, third parties as portfolio, 105–107
Cybersecurity, Project Jasper and, 128

Dai coin, 163
Database
distributed ledger technology *vs.* traditional, 44–47
Townsend Thai, 27–29
Database management
advances in, 10
science of, 169
traditional *vs.* decentralized, 14–15

Data integrity, 15
Data synchronization, 45
Debit cards, 52
Decentralization, 1, 18, 173–174
Decentralized Autonomous Organization (DAO), 11
Decentralized exchange, 137–140
Decentralized ledgers, synchronization of, 8
Decentralized systems, impossibility theorems for, 169
Denison, Erin, 9
Depository Trust and Clearing Corporation (DDTCC), 6–7
Design issues
delegation of portfolios to third party, 105–107
partitioned ledgers, 103–105
permissioned private ledgers, 111–113
private *vs.* public and the role of tokens, 107–111
Developing countries, building financial infrastructure in, 115. *See also* Emerging markets
Diamond-Dybvig model, 104, 134–135, 136
Digital Asset, 5, 37, 46, 146
Digital asset, 38
Digital credit providers
in Kenya, 55
in Sweden, 51–52
Digital reserve bank, 20, 163–165
Digital reserve system, 145, 179
Disintermediation, of distributed ledger technology, 8

Distributed computing, advances in, 10
Distributed consensus, 64–68
Distributed ledgers
 as accounts, 13
 applications, 167
 building financial infrastructure on, 115–125
 categorizing transactions on, 39–40
 components of, 13–14
 decentralization and, 1
 financial accounts and, 168
 innovations making use of, 19–20
 payment systems on, 127–132, 175–176
 public information on, 21
 regulation and, 176–177
 role of tokens, 107–108
 security and, 44
 smart contracts on, 79, 83–84
 stocks and flows on, 77
 summary and conclusion, 167–179
 use in village economies, 37
 verification in, 64–65
Distributed ledger technology (DLT), 1
 disintermediation and, 8
 emerging-market economies and, 23
 enhanced measurement and, 43
 financial services and markets and, 2
 for freight shipping, 6
 land-title projects and, 4–5
 multiparty smart contracts and, 106–107
 regulation and use of, 133–143
 repurchase agreements and, 6–7
 risk of using for payments, 3
 TCP/IP and, 7
 traditional database *vs.*, 44–47
 used to create complete financial accounts, 43
Double-entry bookkeeping, 39, 168
Double-spending, Ripple and, 72–73

e-assets as payment devices, 140
Economics
 computer science *vs.*, 17
 incentives in, 93–102
 trust in, 88–91, 93
Economy
 function of, 24–25
 meaning of, 23, 24
 technology tied to, 25
e-credit, 132
Electronic clearing systems, 52
Emerging markets, 23
 limited financial infrastructure in, 115–116
 use of paper currency in, 15, 42, 49–51
e-messages, 13, 15, 169–170
e-money, 15
 shortages faced by broker-dealers, 56–57
 social gains and, 53–56
Encryption, 59–75
 Algorand, 75
 Bitcoin, 68–71
 contemporary, 63–64

historical examples of, 59–63
HotStuff, 74
Ripple, 71–73
Stellar, 73–75
validated and distributed consensus, 64–68
Endowments, of agent, 24
e-payments, 15
e-securities, 140
e-systems, consensus and, 15–16
Ether cryptocurrency, 11, 163
Ethereum, 6, 17
computing costs, 95, 96–97
contract validation in, 160
cost of decentralization on, 173
Project Jasper and, 127, 128
proof of work and, 65–66, 78
smart contracts and, 67
Ethereum Classic, 11
e-tokens, 140, 170
e-transfers, 13, 52, 169–170
crytography and, 170–171
EvryNet, 20, 124–125, 133, 175

Fabric, 67
Facebook, 161
Facts on ledgers, 77
Fault tolerance, 66–67, 98
Federal Reserve Bank, 6, 109, 111, 164–165
Federal Reserve Bank of Boston, 42–43, 148
Federated Byzantine Agreement (FBA), 66, 67, 73
Fiat money
cryptocurrencies and, 178–179
exchange in Lightnet, 127, 130–132
history of, 148
media of exchange by, 22
multiple-country, 185n4
role of tokens relative to fungibility of, 145–146
value of, 151–155, 179
velocity of, 147, 148
Fiat tokens, 71–72, 149
Financial accounts. *See also* Ledgers as financial accounts
digital ledgers and, 168
as ledgers, 38–40
schemata of agent interaction and, 25, 26
Financial infrastructure, building on distributed ledgers, 115–125
Financial liberalization, tariffs *vs.*, 40–41
Financial service providers, competition among, 124
Financial services and markets
distributed ledger technology and, 2
EvryNet, 124–125
general equilibrium perspective on provision of, 122–124
mitigating runs on, 133–135
transaction time lines in, 5
Fingerprint, 63
Finite-horizon model, 156
Fischer Consensus Problem of distributed computing, 45–46
Fixed objective, communication protocol and, 99–100, 101
Flow, 77
Flow of funds accounts, 41
Fractional reserve banking, Safaricom and, 56

Freight shipping, distributed ledger technology for, 6
Frequency of use in payment, money and, 147–148
Front-loading, 106–107, 174
Full commitment, 88–89, 171
Fundamental welfare theorem, 158–159

General equilibrium perspective on provision of financial services, 122–124
General equilibrium theory, 11, 135–136
Generalized statements of liquidity accounts in the US, 42–43
Generations, model of money and overlapping, 155
Ghost currencies, 150
Government village fund intervention (Thai Baht Fund), 19, 117–118, 174
Grain, as medium of exchange, 148

Hacking events, 11, 44, 58
Hash, cryptographic, 97
Hashing, 63, 68, 70–71
Hawaladars, 72
Hawala system, 72
Helix Institute of Digital Finance, 57
Hold-up problem, 92
Honest nodes, in Bitcoin, 69
Hong Kong Monetary Authority, 5
HotStuff, 16, 74
Households running small and medium-sized enterprises (SMEs) and, 25

Hybrid model of positive token values, 157–158
Hybrid smart-contract systems, 16
Hyperledger, 6, 66, 67
Hyperledger Fabric, 47

IBM, 6, 7, 64
ICRISAT, 148
Immutability of smart contracts, 82
Implementation costs for smart contracts, 94–95
Incentive compatibility, 171
Incentives
  full commitment *vs.*, 88–89
  mechanism design and, 172
  to tell truth in messages, 87
  in validation, 93–102
Income, money transactions and, 154
Income distribution, paying interest and, 153–154
Income statement, 27
  accrued income concept and, 39
  changes in balance sheet and, 39
  creation of financial statements and, 38
  in village economies, 31, 33–34
Indemnity, community-level insurance and, 121
India
  media of exchange in, 148
  TReDS in, 5
Inefficiency, testing for, 155–156
Inflation, 154, 163

Information. *See also* Private information
  private monies and, 140–143
  public, 21, 137
Information asymmetry, 112
Innovation
  Bitcoin and, 4
  context and, 4
  EvryNet example, 124–125
  invention *vs.*, 4, 10
  localization and, 4
  public sector and, 182n7
  smart contracts and, 6
Insurance
  community-level, 120–121
  multiparty insurance agreement, 90–91
  multi-period, principal-agent problem, 85–87
  smoothing economy and, 154
Integrated financial accounts, 27
Integration, 17
Interbank payments, Project Jasper, 127–129
Interbank transfer system, Ripple as, 71–72
Interest
  distribution of income and paying, 153–154
  token values and, 145
Interest rate, digital reserve banks and, 163–165
Intermediation, connectedness and, 9
InterPlanetary File System (IPFS), 97
Invention, 4, 10
iOlite, 94

Kenya. *See* M-Pesa
Keys
  to Bitcoin, 69
  public-private, 64, 79
  to smart contracts, 80–81
Kinship
  Million Baht Fund and, 118
  risk-sharing on basis of, 117
Kraken, 58

Land-title projects, distributed ledger technology and, 4–5
Latency, 45, 47, 67, 135, 177
Ledgers as financial accounts, 31–47
  counterfactual policy analysis, 41–42
  distributed ledger technology *vs.* traditional database, 44–47
  financial accounts as ledgers, 38–40
  generalized statements of liquidity accounts in the US, 42–43
  smart contracts and, 93
  statement of cash flow and balance sheet as ledger, 31–38
  use of village and community-level financial accounts, 40–41
Letters of credit, 119
Liabilities, measurement of, 38–39
Libra, 16, 74, 161
Lightnet, 20, 127, 130–132, 158, 159–160, 165, 176
Lightning Network, 46–47, 169
Limited commitment, 171–172
  trust *vs.*, 88–91

Limited-commitment contract, 89–91
Liquidity
  cash flow statements and, 36
  common concerns about, 56–58
  distributed ledger technology and study of, 36, 43
  Ostroy-Starr model and, 139–140
  productivity *vs.*, 39
  public debt and, 153
  reserve bank, 165
Liquidity accounts for multiple media of exchange, 40–41
Liveness, 67
Loans, community information on who should get, 121–122
Localization, innovation and, 4

Maersk platform, 6, 7, 146
MakerDAO, 161
Malicious leaders, Algorand and, 75
Malicious nodes, 172
Marginal rates of substitution, digital reserve banks and, 164
Markov perfect equilibrium, 70
Measurement
  of economic activity, 27
  of liabilities, 38–39
Mechanism design, 12–13, 171–172
  Corda and, 78
  cryptocurrencies and, 178
  key elements from, 82
  meaning of trust in, 88–91
  mitigating runs on banks and markets and, 134
  smart contracts and, 81–93
  tokens and, 21–22, 145–146, 150–151
Mesh networks, 47, 74
Mesopotamians, cryptography and, 59–62, 171
Messages
  encryption of, 63–64
  limited space, 88
  single period contract with, 82
  in smart contracts, 81–83, 97–102
  verification of, 170–171
Metadata on distributed ledger, 39
Microdata on transactions, 165
Micropayments, Stellar and, 5–6
Million Baht Fund (Thailand), 19, 117–118, 174
Miners, Bitcoin, 68–70, 92
Mint, 43
Monetary Authority of Singapore, 129, 184n3
Monetary exchange, Turnpike model of, 152
Monetary models, interest rate policy for digital reserve banks, 163–165
Monetary policy, role of liquidity in, 58
Monetary solution, Ostroy-Starr model and, 139
Monetary theory
  cryptocurrencies and, 178
  lessons for regulation of payment systems from, 137–143
  Walrasian, competitive markets, 151–156

Money. *See also* Fiat money; Paper currency
  contracts and, 25
  cryptocurrency and value of, 158–160
  definitions of, 145, 147–148
  e-money, 15, 53–57
  endogenous valuation of, 152–155, 157–158
  exogenous valuation of, 156–157
  in Ostroy-Starr model, 138
  as store of value, 153, 154
  types of, 21
  as unit of account, 153
  value of, 22, 145, 156–157
Money good, 139
Money markets, Thai village, 116–117, 174
"Moneyness," velocity and, 21
Money transfer operator (MTO), 20, 130–132, 158, 176
Moral hazard, 85, 86–87, 135
M-Pesa, 15, 53–56, 170
  liquidity shortages and, 56–57
  operational flows of, 54
  social value of, 55
  as stable coin, 54–55
  transfers and borrowing/lending among Safaricom agents, 57
M-Shwari, 55
Multiparty insurance agreement, 90–91
Multiparty mechanisms, in contracts, 13–14
Multi-period, principal-agent insurance problem, 85–87
Multi-period contracts, 82

Multiple colored tokens, 107, 109–111, 150, 174
Multiple-country fiat monies, 185n4
Multiple media of exchange, 147, 148–150, 178
  liquidity accounts and, 40–41
Multiple media of exchange equilibria, 140–143

Nakamoto, Satoshi, 9, 10, 44, 69, 70
Nash equilibrium, 81, 92, 134, 177
National currencies, e-money systems for, 71
National income and product accounts (NIPA), 41
National income data, 155–156
Natural discount rate, digital reserve banks, 164
Netting, 128, 175–176
Nodes
  incentives to validate correctly, 91
  malicious, 98, 101
  notaries and, 80, 175
  smart contract, 78–79, 80
  trusted or not, 17, 93
Novelty, complexity *vs.*, 3

"Off-chain" environment, 169
Office for National Statistics (ONS) Economic Expert Working Group (EEWG), 43
OmiseGO, 58
Opaque computational systems, 64
Open-source banking services, 20, 124, 175

Oracle, 79
Ostroy-Starr model, 137–140
Over-the-counter (OTC) markets, 47, 138
Over-the-counter (OTC) trade in securities, 104

Panel Study of Income Dynamics (PSID), 43
Paper checks, 148, 149
Paper currency
  transactions recorded as ledgers, 31, 36
  use in Thailand, 15, 42, 49–51
Pareto criterion, 11, 123
Pareto optimal allocation, 24, 137, 142
Parties to contract, 78
Partition agents, risk-sharing arrangements for, 47
Partitioned ledgers, 103–105
  colored coins and, 110
  concealment and, 104–106
  contract node and, 173–174
Partition tolerance, distributed ledgers and, 45
Payment matrix, 147–148
Payments, waterfall, 119
Payments Canada white paper, 127, 128
Payment systems, lessons from monetary theory for regulation of, 137–143
Payment systems on distributed ledgers, 3, 127–132
  Lightnet and Velo, 127, 130–132
  Project Jasper, 127–129, 175–176

Payoff, smart contract, 85
Payout, insurance, 120–121
PayPal, 89
Permissioned blockchains, 46–47, 66
Permissioned private ledgers, 103–105, 111–113
  Project Jasper and, 127–129
Physical tokens, 174
Planner
  contract node as, 174
  of mechanism design, 12–13
"Planner" problem of mechanism, 173
Political economy of reform, 12
Portfolios, delegation to third party, 105–107
Postal Pay, 55
Practical Byzantine Fault Toleration (PBFT) algorithms, 66, 74–75
Price-fixing schemes, cryptocurrencies and, 162–163
Private blockchains, 46
Private clearinghouses, private and public ownership of, 13
Private debt, 140–143, 149, 177–178
Private information
  letting be public, 98
  Ostroy-Starr model and, 139
  partitioned ledgers and, 103–105
  smart contracts and, 83–84
  tokens and, 111–112
Private monies, information problem with, 140–143
Process synchronization, 45
Productivity, liquidity *vs.*, 39

Products/systems, valuation of, 12
Project Jasper, 20, 127–129, 175–176
Promise-keeping, 86–87
Proof of stake (PoS), 66, 171
Proof of work (PoW), 16, 65–66, 67, 78, 171
Propy.com, 5
Protocol, 58
Public and private partnerships (PPPs) in Sweden, 182n7
Public debt, liquidity and, 153
Public information, on distributed ledgers, 21, 137
Public ledgers, regulation and, 177
Public-private keys, 64, 79
Public sector, innovations and, 182n7

Quorum, 66, 67–68

R3, 6, 66, 128
Randomization, partitioned ledgers and, 104–105, 173–174
Rebalancing, in developing countries, 57
Reconciliation, in Lightnet, 131
Regulation and use of distributed ledger technology, 20, 133–143, 176–177
  limits of competition for contracts, 135–137
  mitigating runs on banks and markets, 133–135
  need for coordination of payment systems, 138–143
Rehypothecation of collateral, 141
Relationships, smart contracts and enduring, 83–84
"Relayers," 47
Remittances in Southeast Asia, 5–6, 130–132, 176
Reneging, 172
Renegotiation, 94
Repo transaction, 161–162
Repurchase agreements, digital ledger technology and, 6–7
Reputation, smart contracts and, 91–92
Reserve bank liquidity, 165
Retrading, 136–137
Revelation principle, 81, 97
Riksbank, 51–52, 182n1
Ripple, 6, 16
  cryptography and, 71–73
  Federated Byzantine Agreement and, 66
  validation system of, 8
Ripple Protocol Consensus Algorithm, 73
Risk aversion, information disclosure and, 112
Risk sharing, 19, 55, 116–117, 174
Rotating savings and credit association (ROSCA) transactions, 50
RTGS (real-time gross settlement) system, 184n3
Runs on banks and markets, mitigating, 133–135

Safaricom, 15, 54, 55–56, 170
Safety, in encryption, 67
Savings
  difference between revenues and expenses, 38
  mechanism design and, 150–151

Savings/investment account, 41
Savings products, 120
Secrets, permissioned private ledgers and, 111–113
Secure Hash Algorithm SHA-256, 63
Securities
  e-securities, 140
  as payment devices, 140–141
  tokenized, 146, 148
Security, distributed ledgers and, 44
Seigniorage-style algorithm, 162
Sequential-service models, 134
Shocks, 153
  back- and front-loading, 174
  customer needs and, 104
  sharing risk to mitigate, 116–117
  smart contracts and, 83, 105
  tokens and, 18
Small and medium-sized enterprises (SMEs), in Thailand, 25, 51, 116
Smart contracts, 16, 77–81
  blockchain platforms and, 67
  capabilities of, 80
  coding and implementation costs, 94–97
  in computer sciences, 93–102
  costly state verification, 88
  distributed ledger technology and, 175
  economics of collusion, 92
  EvryNet and, 124–125
  examples, 119–122
  impact of enduring relationships and, 83–84
  implementation through sequential play, 92–93
  incentives to take appropriate action, 85–87
  innovation and, 6
  lack of immutability in, 11
  ledgers of the financial accounts, 93
  Lightnet and, 160
  limits of competition for, 135–137
  meaning of trust, 88–91
  mechanism design, 81–93
  messages, 81–83
  multi-period, 82
  payoff, 85
  promised utility as the state, 85
  reliability of messages, 97–102
  reputation and, 91–92
  schematic of financial accounts and agent interaction through, 25, 26
  Seigniorage-style algorithm and, 162
  summary of, 172–174
  utility threats, 87–88
  value of tokens and, 145
Social gains, e-money and, 53–56
Social security, money and, 154–155
Southeast Asia (SEA). *See also* Thailand
  innovations in, 175
  limited financial infrastructure in emerging markets in, 115–116
  money transfer operators in, 176
  remittances in, 5–6, 130–132, 176

Spot-trade condition, quid pro quo, 138
Stable coins, 160–163, 179
Star communication network, 74
State, promised utility as the, 85
Statement of cash flow in village economies, 31, 36–38
State of the system, 77
Stellar, 5–6, 8, 16, 66, 131, 132, 149
Stellar Consensus Protocol (SCP), 73
Stellar Development Foundation, 73–75
Stock, 77
Strategic reliability, 102
Supermartingales/submartingales, Bitcoin prices and, 159
Survey of Consumer Finances (SCF), 43
Sweden
 as cashless society, 15, 51–52
 currency infrastructure in, 182n1
 currency to GDP ratio, 52, 169
 public and private partnerships in, 182n7
Swift, 66
Swish, 51, 182n7
Synchronization of data and processes, 45
Synchronous systems, 14–15

Tally sticks, 62–63, 149, 171, 183n1
Tally stock, 62
Tariffs, real and financial liberalization vs., 40–41

Taxes
 digital reserve banks and, 164
 value of money and payment of, 156–157
TCP/IP (transmission control protocol/internet protocol), 7, 59
Technological change to fill in the gaps, 9–10
Technology
 agent access to, 24
 difficulty of adopting transformative, 3
 distributed ledger technology and, 2
 ties of economy to, 25
Tether, 161
Thailand. *See also* Townsend Thai project
 change in policy in, 42
 currency to GDP ratio, 49, 169
 e-money *vs.* paper currency in, 15
 Lightnet in, 130–132
 Million Baht Fund, 19, 117–118, 174
 use of paper currency in, 15, 42, 49–51
Thin markets, 57
Third party, delegation of portfolios to, 105–107. *See also* Trusted third party
Third-party custodian, 174
Time lines
 of events within given period under contract, 27, 28
 schemata of financial accounts and agent interaction through smart contracts, 25, 26

Tokens, 18, 74. *See also* Coins
  achieving unique consensus and, 108–109
  as communication devices, 109
  fiat, 71–72, 149
  hybrid model of positive token values, 157–158
  interdeterminacy of value, 22
  mechanism design for, 150–151
  Mesopotamian, 59–62
  multiple colored, 107, 109–111, 150, 174
  physical, 174
  private information and, 111–112
  private *vs.* public and role of, 107–111
  public verified histories of, 111
  removing indeterminancy of values, 159–160
  role and value of, 21–22
  role relative to fiat money fungibility, 145–146
  taxation and, 164
  tokenized securities and, 146, 148
  as units of account, 150
  utility, 146, 156, 160, 179
  value of, 145
Townsend Thai project, 13, 167
  data for study of financial access, 19, 27–29, 49
  national income and product accounts, 40–41
  sharing of risk to mitigate shocks, 116–118, 174
  transaction log, 31, 36–37
Trade credit, 149

Trade Information Warehouse, 7
Trade receivables, TReDS and, 5
Trades
  history of, on immutable ledger, 177
  token system to keep track of, 109, 111
Transaction costs, 24
Transaction log, in Thai village economies, 31, 36
Transaction speed, encryption and, 67
Transaction time lines, 5
TReDS, 5
Trust
  borrowing and lending and, 89
  Byzantine protocols with, 16
  distributed ledger technology and alleviation of limitation of, 118
  in economics, 88–91, 93
  financial system and, 170–171
  implemented by "scoring," 91–92
  mechanism design and, 171–172
Trusted third party
  central banks as, 9
  contracts and, 171
  decentralized systems and, 169
  M-Pesa and, 15, 170
  reputations of, 91
  Safaricom as, 55, 56
  security and, 44
  speed and cost and, 46
Trust lines, in Ripple, 72
Turnpike model of monetary exchange, 152

Unique consensus, 78, 108–109
United States
    economic surveys in, 43
    generalized statements of liquidity accounts, 42–43
    impact of tariffs in, 40, 42
    liquidity management in, 57–58
    multiple media of exchange in, 148
Unit of account, money as, 153
Universal Market Access (UMA), 6
Utility threats, smart contracts and, 87–88
Utility tokens, 146, 156, 160, 179

Validation
    alternative, 67–68
    bad actors and, 67
    of code, 17
    distributed consensus and, 64–68
    incentives in, 93–102
    in Ripple network, 72–73
    in Stellar protocol, 73
Validators, in Bitcoin, 69–70
Validity consensus, 78
Velocity
    of fiat money, 147, 148
    "moneyness" and, 21
    private debt and, 149
Velo Labs, 20
Velo network, 176

Velo tokens
    exchanges of, 184n4
    Lightnet and, 130–132, 158, 159–160
Verification, costly state, 88
Village economies (Thailand)
    balance of payments account, 40–41
    statement of cash flow and balance sheet as ledger, 31–33, 36
    use of distributed ledgers, 37–38
Villages. *See also* Townsend Thai project
    Million Baht Fund and, 19, 117–118, 174

Walmart, distributed ledger technology and supply chain tracking and, 6, 146
Walrasian allocation, 138
Walrasian competitive markets, 150, 151–156
Walrasian equilibrium, 135, 137
Walrasian optimum, 177
Waterfall payment, 119
Welfare metric, 11

XRP coin, 71

Zero-knowledge-proof systems, 64
0x, 58